The Modern School Practices Series

COLLEGE OF EDUCATION   UNIVERSITY OF MINNESOTA

EDUCATION AND THE CREATIVE POTENTIAL

Number 5 in the Modern School Practices Series

COLLEGE OF EDUCATION · BUREAU OF EDUCATIONAL RESEARCH

THE MODERN SCHOOL PRACTICES SERIES · NUMBER FIVE

Education and the Creative Potential

E. PAUL TORRANCE

THE UNIVERSITY OF MINNESOTA PRESS, Minneapolis

PUBLISHED IN GREAT BRITAIN, INDIA, AND PAKISTAN BY THE OXFORD UNIVERSITY PRESS,
LONDON, BOMBAY, AND KARACHI, AND IN CANADA BY THOMAS ALLEN, LTD., TORONTO

PREFACE

CONTINUED requests for copies of the papers on the Minnesota Studies of Creative Thinking which I have presented before various groups, and for the reports of the earlier exploratory studies on which some of these papers were based, have influenced the Bureau of Educational Research to publish this collection of seven papers and six experimental studies. In my selection I have attempted to cover a wide range of topics of general interest and to include materials not contained in my book, *Guiding Creative Talent* (Prentice-Hall, Inc., 1962).

Although originally presented at a conference of Minnesota leaders in education, the first chapter — "The Creative Potential of School Children in the Space Age" — is equally relevant to the teacher, counselor or guidance worker, or other educational specialist. Challenging educators to engage in frontier thinking, to acquaint themselves with recent research and experimentation on the creative potential of school children, this chapter calls for changes in educational objectives, examines some recent breakthroughs in the measurement of creative thinking abilities, and introduces the concept of the creative teacher-pupil relationship.

"Conditions for Creative Growth" summarizes the results of research into the conditions that facilitate or inhibit creativity, directing its message not only to teachers but to administrators, counselors, and parents, who all have an important role in creating the conditions that encourage creative growth.

Though originally prepared for a national meeting of school psychologists, "Mental Health Problems of Highly Creative Children" examines cases that are also of interest to teachers, administrators, counselors, and parents. A general theory explaining the nature of the mental health problems of highly creative persons as a form of divergency is also attempted.

"Giving Children a Chance to Learn and Think Creatively" is aimed more directly at parents than the other chapters in developing the concept of learning creatively as opposed to learning by authority, a concept that is also of special concern to teachers, and describes how parents and teachers sometimes tend to interfere with the functioning of the creative thinking abilities. The need for cooperation between the school and the home is emphasized.

"Creative Students in Our Schools Today" shows how the creative can be identified both through test and nontest methods and presents some of the problems in identifying and guiding them. Generalizations based on large-scale research show in what way the cases presented are prototypes rather than unique. Educators are challenged to forge ahead with the retooling needed to provide appropriate educational opportunities for realizing the creative potential.

Using data from several different cultures, the sixth chapter — "Cultural Discontinuities and the Development of Originality" — argues that the decrements in the measured creative thinking abilities and in creative behavior, observed at about ages five, nine, thirteen, and seventeen, are greatly influenced if not determined by the different ways in which the culture treats the curiosity and the creative needs of children and youth. Cultural discontinuities are discussed as a major source of personality disturbances that inhibit creative behavior of almost every type.

"Religious Education and Creative Thinking" reiterates the point that man's natural inclination is to learn creatively; many things, including beliefs, can be learned more effectively and economically if learned creatively rather than by authority alone. By placing greater emphasis on learning creatively, we can greatly improve the quality of religious education.

Of the six exploratory studies in Part II, originally issued as mimeographed reports, the first two were conducted as experiments for use in devising tests and testing procedures for studying the development of the creative thinking abilities. The first was designed to clarify the problem of selecting sexually appropriate test tasks. As it turned out, we discovered that highly creative children are frequently skillful in restructuring tasks which they consider inappropriate to their sex in order to deal with them creatively, and that in the second and third grades boys are superior to girls on problems such as the toy-improvement task. The second of these studies confirms the importance of manipulation in generating inventive ideas.

In the third study, use of a laboratory model of heterogeneous groups based on measures of creative thinking allowed us to study at first hand how groups treat their most creative members, how they use negative sanctions even at the sacrifice of group success, and how the creative cope with group pressures.

That deliberate methods for increasing creativity can be used with children in the primary grades is suggested in the fourth study. The fifth, showing how social changes affect the attitudes of children concerning the areas in which it is legitimate for them to inquire and to enjoy inquiry, suggests that the relative value placed upon the ideas of boys versus girls by their peers in performing science tasks is slow to change. The final study reports results of research with adult samples on the problems of sex-role identification and creative thinking.

For supporting the research out of which this book has grown, I am indebted to the Cooperative Research Program of the United States Office of Education, the Hill Family Foundation, the University of Minnesota Graduate School Research Fund, and the College of Education. I am especially grateful to the staff of the Bureau of Educational Research, to the schools which cooperated in our experimental studies, and to all who served as subjects.

E. PAUL TORRANCE, *Director*
Bureau of Educational Research

July, 1962

TABLE OF CONTENTS

PART I. GENERAL PROBLEMS

"To give a fair chance to potential creativity is a matter of life and death for any society."

ARNOLD TOYNBEE, "Has America Neglected Its Creative Minority?" *California Monthly*, February 1962

THE CREATIVE POTENTIAL OF SCHOOL CHILDREN
IN THE SPACE AGE

As WE enter the Space Age, we hear a great deal from the critics of American education, and perhaps even more from its defenders. In my view, however, the creative challenge to education in the coming years will be met by neither critics nor defenders, but by prophets and frontier thinkers. As an educational researcher, I propose to play the role of prophet in this paper. Though fear of being tagged "witchdoctor" or "soothsayer" makes us shrink from assuming this role, we educators must increasingly become prophets. To behave effectively in his universe, man must improve wherever possible his ability to predict the consequences of a given course of action. As a scientist, I take courage from the fact that science has done more than any other human activity to improve man's gift of prophecy.

The Space Age is taking us places where old and comfortable ideas no longer apply. Much will be required of the creative potential of today's school children. Threats to man's survival challenge us to consider what man may become, at his best, and to search for new ways of helping children realize this creative potential. "We know not what man may become." But there is no evidence that human evolution is drawing to its close. Because of the continued development of man's thinking, his creative thinking, I suspect that the man of the 1960's will appear to be as naive and brutish to future generations as the cave man seems to us.

Evolution of this creative man will require changes in education: changes as radical as the technological shifts that are causing them; changes that require boldness, imagination, and hard work. Wishing will not bring them about. Just as self-hypnotism has not enabled man to project himself into space, we cannot achieve the required conditions for progress in education by thinking happy thoughts. However, if re-

NOTE: This chapter was originally a paper presented at the Education and Space Age Conference of the Minnesota Chapter of the Air Force Association, University of Minnesota, May 7, 1960.

3

sponse to our research from educators all over the United States is any indication, some truly profound changes in American education are taking shape today.

One of the most revolutionary changes I foresee is a revision of the objectives of education. Today we proclaim that our schools exist for learning. We say that we must get tougher and make pupils learn more. Schools of the future will be designed not only for *learning* but for *thinking*. More and more insistently, today's schools and colleges are being asked to produce men and women who can think, who can make new scientific discoveries, who can find more adequate solutions to impelling world problems, who cannot be brainwashed, men and women who can adapt to change and maintain sanity in this age of acceleration. This is the creative challenge to education.

We are slow to modify educational objectives. Colleges and universities are still teaching only the *psychology of learning*, almost never the *psychology of thinking*. Teachers of the near future are still being taught only how to construct tests to assess what pupils learn, almost never to determine what pupils can do with what they learn. Teachers state objectives in the language of learning — especially in terms of the pupils' being familiar with and conforming to behavioral norms, and learning the "right" attitudes. Rarely do teachers state objectives in terms of thinking — I mean thinking of all kinds — critical, creative, constructive, independent, logical, liberal, and analytical. Their methods, the tasks they assign pupils, the relationships they establish with children — all are calculated to produce learning. Rarely do they stimulate learners to leap the barrier from learning to thinking. Most of our educational research is still being devoted to the investigation of the learning process; seldom to the thinking process.

One indication of the slowness of change is reflected in our recent study for the Minnesota State Advisory Committee for Social Studies (Torrance and Ross, 1961). A questionnaire sent to a random sample of elementary and secondary social science teachers asked them to name a subject or unit they teach in social studies and then list what they considered the three most important objectives of this subject or unit. Each objective was then classified according to the type of mental operation pupils would have to engage in to achieve it.

There are five of these operations (Guilford, 1959a): cognition, memory, convergent behavior, divergent thinking, and evaluation. Under *cognition* we placed objectives that require pupils to recognize, be familiar with, be aware of, know about, learn about, appreciate, and the like. Under *memory* we included remembering, knowing thoroughly, and acquiring knowledge. Under *convergent behavior* we placed objectives requiring conformity to behavioral norms, the proper or "right" attitude, the correct solution. Under *divergent thinking* were independent thinking, constructive thinking, creative thinking, original work, questioning, inquiring, and similar activities. *Evaluation* included critical thinking, assessing, evaluating, judging, making decisions, comparing and contrasting.

Table 1. Frequency and Percentage of Types of Mental Operations Named as Most Important by Teachers of Elementary Social Studies, Secondary Social Studies, and Elementary Language Arts

Type of Mental Operation	Elementary Social Studies		Secondary Social Studies		Elementary Language Arts	
	N	%	N	%	N	%
Cognition	762	76.7	855	65.9	14	24.6
Memory	55	5.4	68	5.2	2	3.5
Convergent behavior....	169	16.5	265	20.5	33	57.9
Divergent thinking......	9	0.9	30	2.3	5	8.8
Evaluation	5	0.5	79	6.1	3	5.2
Total	1,000	100.0	1,297	100.0	57	100.0
Nonrespondents	38	9.7	19	4.3	...	...
Number in sample....	390		443		20	

The results presented in Table 1 show that an overwhelming majority of the social studies objectives fall into the cognitive category — over 70 per cent for the entire sample. Most of the remaining objectives require conformity to the behavioral norms — about 17 per cent at the elementary level and about 21 per cent at the secondary level. Eliminating the five per cent that require memory, precious few remain for either of the thinking categories.

Although these results were obtained from a study conducted for a group interested in improving social studies education, social studies teachers will probably be one of the slowest groups to respond to the creative challenge to education, because the greater changes in approach and technique are taking place in mathematics, science, English and language arts, foreign languages, home economics, and art education.

Mathematics provides perhaps the best example of what will happen in other fields. Already familiar are such exciting textbooks as *Exploring Numbers, New Thinking with Numbers,* and *Adventure with Numbers*. At the University of Minnesota we have been observing with interest the experimental work of the National Laboratory for the Improvement of Secondary School Mathematics. Recently, Professor Paul Rosenbloom permitted me to analyze a set of daily logs submitted by teachers participating in this experiment. These logs, describing both teacher and pupil activities, were submitted during 1958–1959 by the five least and five most effective teachers in terms of pupils' achievement in proportion to aptitude. The same scheme we had applied to the social studies objectives was used in classifying these activities. The results in Table 2 present a striking contrast to the social studies data. The most effective mathematics teachers report far more *thinking* activities for their pupils than the least effective teachers. Compared with social studies teachers, however, even the least effective mathematics teachers appear to be more concerned about stimulating their pupils to leap the barrier between learning and thinking.

Table 2. Frequency and Percentage of Types of Mental Operations of Pupils Described by Five Most and Five Least Effective Mathematics Teachers

Type of Mental Operation	Five Most Effective Teachers		Five Least Effective Teachers	
	N	%	N	%
Cognition	29	10.8	128	33.9
Memory	23	8.6	35	9.3
Convergent behavior	86	32.0	98	25.9
Divergent thinking.............	98	36.4	78	20.6
Evaluation	33	12.3	39	10.3

NOTE: Chi-square $= 51.56$: $P < .001$.

Although study after study (Guilford, 1959b; Taylor, 1960; Wallace, 1961) indicates that some of the abilities involved in creative thinking and decision making are vital to vocational success, there are many powerful reasons why elementary and secondary teachers are reluctant to give attention to the development of these abilities. These teachers feel the domination of our colleges. We become aware of this domination and of the problems it involves when we analyze the admissions tests used by outstanding colleges and universities. One analysis reveals that the majority of test items require only the exercise of cognitive abilities. There are signs, however, that changes are already taking place. Recently, a representative of the National Merit Scholarship Corporation called me, asking for permission to use an instrument I devised some years ago for assessing risk-taking tendencies or ability to test one's limits. Their test battery already includes indicators of certain creative achievements. Among their scholars, those labeled highly creative but not top scorers on measures of scholastic aptitude are succeeding as well or better than those scoring highest on traditional scholastic measures but not so high on the measure of creative thinking. Flanagan (1959) and his associates are using a test of ingenuity in their national talent survey. I understand that other test development agencies plan to include measures of creative thinking ability in their college admission batteries.

THE BOLD, ADVENTUROUS SEARCH FOR NEW WAYS

If changed objectives are to mean anything, many other new developments are necessary — in teaching methods, in curriculum and instruction materials, in identifying talent, and in evaluating achievement. A large-scale reorganization, a complete retooling is required, without which we stand in danger of creating more anachronisms. To achieve our changed objectives we must invest in the future through educational research. To reap the fruits of this research, educators must learn to apply results and to consult those who understand the real processes of learning and thinking. Schools of the future must encourage and welcome criticism and use it in the search for new ways.

One promising development is our expansion of the concept of mental abilities, of which traditional tests of intelligence (IQ tests) measure only a few, primarily cognition and memory. I believe the evidence is clear that children *can* be taught to use creative thinking abilities in acquiring even traditional school learnings, that traditional concepts of under- and over-achievement are woefully outmoded, that the learning procedures of highly creative children are quite different from those of children with high IQ's but without high creative thinking ability, and that many social pressures interfere with the development and expression of these abilities.

These findings are dramatically illustrated in a study recently conducted in the University of Minnesota Elementary School. We differentiated the highly creative children (as identified by our tests) from the highly intelligent ones (as identified by an individually administered intelligence test). The highly creative group ranked in the upper 20 per cent of their classes on creativity but not on intelligence. The highly intelligent group ranked in the upper 20 per cent on intelligence but not on creativity. (I should add parenthetically that regardless of the measure of IQ or scholastic aptitude used, and regardless of the educational level, about 70 per cent of the top 20 per cent on creativity would have been excluded from gifted groups selected on the basis of IQ alone.)

Although the average difference between these two groups is over 25

IQ points, there are no statistically significant differences in any of the achievement measures used (Gates Reading Test and Iowa Tests of Basic Skills). The highly intelligent children, however, were described by their teachers as more desirable pupils, more intimately known, more ambitious, and more hardworking or studious. In other words, the highly creative child learns as much as the highly intelligent child without appearing to work as hard. My guess is that these highly creative children are learning and thinking when they appear to be "fooling around," even when they engage in forbidden manipulative and exploratory activities.

These findings suggest the need for tests of the creative thinking abilities. Research and experimental programs are already using a variety of testing instruments which permit us to study the development of creativeness. Before long, these tests will become available for use in much the same way as tests of intelligence are now used. Examinations assessing achievement of skills in creative thought will be developed in almost all subjects, following the principles now being used in developing ability tests.

The introduction of these instruments of study provides a breakthrough in our search for new ways. We can now discover how the creative thinking abilities develop from kindergarten through graduate school, what impedes their development at various stages, what influences contribute to their growth, what role they play in vocational success and in coping with life's daily stresses.

Most of these abilities develop rapidly from kindergarten through the third grade, with boys tending to excel girls. Between the third and fourth grades a sharp decrement occurs, with boys falling below girls. There are gains in the fifth and sixth grades, another drop in the seventh, and growth through the eighth, ninth, tenth, and eleventh grades. Through research, educators will gradually achieve an understanding of the reasons for the severe decrements in the fourth and seventh grades; the factors contributing to recovery or nonrecovery will be identified; and the means of preventing highly talented children from needlessly sacrificing their creative talent will be found.

Already we have demonstrated that the quantity and quality of ideas produced by children can be improved by teaching them a few principles for thinking of ideas, by providing "warm-up" activities, by competition, and by varying the instructions given in assigning tasks. Experiments now in progress will demonstrate that teachers in service can be taught to apply these and other principles so as to bring about measurable differences in the development of the pupils' thinking abilities.

Some of the more obvious blocks to the thinking processes are becoming clear. These include premature attempts to eliminate fantasy; restrictions on manipulativeness and curiosity; overemphasis or misplaced emphasis on sex roles; overemphasis on prevention, fear, and timidity; misplaced emphasis on certain verbal skills; emphasis on destructive criticism; and coercive pressures from peers.

The Creative Teacher-Pupil Relationship. Our adventurous search will be concerned, too, with the teacher-pupil relationship. Thinking processes are automatic, swift and spontaneous when not disturbed by other influences. The trouble is that our relationships with children and the structure of the school situation interfere with this natural process. In the future, we must give youngsters sufficient opportunity to bridge the gap between learning and thinking.

How can teachers avoid jamming the brakes on the creative velocity of a child's thinking apparatus and driving it "off course" (Kubie, 1958, p. 105)? Psychologists and psychiatrists have provided us with some extremely useful insights concerning these inhibiting educational influences (Kubie, 1958; Moreno, 1947; Schafer, 1958). Though we are still confronted with many puzzling paradoxes and dilemmas, recent breakthroughs should enable us to resolve many of them within the next ten or twenty years.

In mulling over these paradoxes and dilemmas, it seems to me that much of the answer lies in the relationship of the teacher and pupil. I call the kind of relationship I have in mind the "creative teacher-pupil relationship."

Most current conceptualizations of the teacher-pupil relationship are reactive ones in which the teacher responds to the stimulations of a particular child and the child responds to the stimulations of a particular teacher. Emphasis is on the correctness both of the stimulus and the response. The *creative* teacher-pupil relationship, however, is *not* a stimulus-response situation, but involves a living relationship, a co-experiencing.

Current research shows that considerable estrangement between highly creative youngsters and their teachers is usual (Getzels and Jackson, 1962; Torrance, 1962). If teachers do not relate well with youngsters who are most outstanding as creative thinkers, we must wonder even more about the detrimental effect of the teacher-pupil relationship on those children who show rather poor ability to think, particularly those with high IQ's. The relationship I visualize will prevent many of the present difficulties because it requires a willingness on the teacher's part to embark on unknown pathways. In contrast to stubbornly retaining the comfort and safety of the time-tested process and the well-traveled pathway, the teacher must be willing to permit one thing to lead to another, must be ready to break out of the mold, rather than look upon children in traditional ways, through stereotyped attitudes, and thus fail to relate to them as real persons.

Because it is so much a matter of *being*, rather than one of acting and being acted upon, errors or mistakes in the creative relationship are often irrelevant (Moustakas, 1959). We have all been puzzled by the success of some rare teacher who has violated almost every rule of good pedagogy. Perhaps the secret is that such teachers maintain the creative relationship. Their errors in form, or what seem to be errors, don't matter.

How does the creative teacher-pupil relationship come about? What can the teacher do to establish such a relationship? It happens in much the same way that creative thought takes place. No matter how much we strain to think of a new idea, however fervently we may want to think of one, our conscious effort may fail altogether. Then it seems to "just happen," as if through preconscious processes, as when the inventor or scientific discoverer is struck by his big idea in church, in the bath tub, or in bed. It requires an openness to experience, a willingness to participate in the relationship once it happens.

To understand more fully and concretely the nature of the creative teacher-pupil relationship, we have been collecting from teachers accounts of actual incidents which describe their efforts to establish creative relationships. These data, rich, exciting, and provocative, provide clues for studying the problem scientifically.

Creative Teaching. Obviously, the changes I have attempted to envision will require creative, adventurous-spirited teachers. Unless we have such teachers, children who dare to imagine, question, and create will continue to be estranged from unsympathetic teachers, the kind who derail the quick, automatic thought processes of their pupils. Not stimulated to think, these children will continue to be robbed of one of learning's most important rewards — namely, thinking. Without creative teachers, creative talent will go unrecognized, undeveloped, and unrewarded. To recruit, supervise, and encourage creative teachers is the coming responsibility of our school administrators. They face a challenging task.

Just as teachers prefer the high IQ pupil to the highly creative one, school administrators prefer less creative teachers to the more creative ones. One recent study (Jex, 1959) showed that the ratings by principals and supervisors of a group of science teachers are negatively and significantly related to their scores on a test of creativity and on tests of their knowledge about the subjects they teach. Just as the highly creative child causes classroom problems, the highly creative teacher generates problems for the school administrator. To be creative is to be unpredictable, and the unpredictable always makes us uneasy. We like to be able to predict because we feel safer, more secure, more in control of things. The uneasiness and uncertainty of the administrator may find expression in feelings and even actions of hostility toward the creative teacher. Furthermore, resentment reflected in the recommendations and ratings received from other administrators concerning candidates is likely to influence one's own recommendations and ratings.

Creative teachers nonetheless need creative supervision. Because they can't stop thinking, these teachers don't stop working with a forty-hour week. The supervisor who cannot tolerate an independent spirit will find it difficult to direct or rigidly channel the energies of the creative teacher, who becomes completely absorbed in his work and sometimes equates supervision with interference. Anyone who tries to suggest a change in the work of a creative person just as he is finishing a job may be inviting an explosion. The work at that point is as much a part of the worker as his vital organs. The best approach is to wait a while. Later, he may be far more willing to make alterations (Ardleigh, 1959).

If we recognize the problems of creative people and understand the reasons behind them, we will find it less difficult to work with them. The truly creative teacher does not work for status or power; he has no desire to be principal or superintendent. He works in order to live with himself: the freedom to create is his greatest reward. Occasionally, he may prefer to work alone; he may insist upon setting his own pace. The mind needs an incubation period of seeming inactivity to hatch ideas. Since creativity involves divergent thinking, we can expect the creative teacher to express ideas which differ from our own and from some of education's time-honored practices. Furthermore, since he cares nought for power, he is unlikely to change his thinking in order to curry favor with his superiors. He may be difficult to hold to routine and become restless under conventional restraint. He works best when dealing with difficult, challenging problems or when engrossed in a project that is his "baby." There will be times when he will defy precedent. He may try a new idea without official permission.

Most creative teachers, however, are worth whatever trouble they cause. There are limits, but the administrator can afford to tolerate a few mistakes. Otherwise, the teacher's fear of failure will prevent his exercising truly creative initiative. At times the administrator or supervisor can buffer his contact with others, with people who just don't understand the creative process. Creative teachers have a breadth of vision; they see relationships between seemingly remote things and bring them together in meaningful ways. Supervisors who make no effort to understand this ability are likely to react with unjust criticism.

School administrators will also need to give attention to rewarding creative efforts among teachers. In time our society will learn how to more effectively reward creativity in almost all fields of work. Today, the creative worker everywhere can scarcely obtain rewards in proportion to his contribution without accepting a position of power, an administrative job. Frequently the demands of the administrative job spell the end of his making a creative contribution. Not that we have no need for creative administrators. We simply have to develop more satisfactory procedures for rewarding creative talent wherever it occurs.

FUTURE CONSEQUENCES

Now that we have tried to envision the future achievements of education in meeting the creative challenge of the Space Age, let us try to envision some of the probable consequences. What "good" will be achieved by changing our objectives? By giving attention to the development of the thinking abilities along with cognition, memory, and conformity to the behavioral norms? By our bold, adventurous search for new ways — new kinds of tests for identifying talent and measuring mental growth, new kinds of teacher-pupil relationships, new kinds of achievement tests, new ways of rewarding creative achievement? By including in teacher education, courses on the *psychology of thinking* and by giving teachers in training experiences in thinking and decision making? What will we gain by recruiting, selecting, and rewarding creative people in the teaching profession?

When we envision changes, we rarely dare think through the consequences. Although the human imagination cannot foresee all the consequences of any action, it is important that we attempt to make our predictions as realistic as possible. In drawing up the balance sheet, we must include the survival of man and certainly the survival of our democratic way of life. From the facts before us, I think we must conclude that survival requires that the creative potential of today's and tomorrow's school children be developed and used.

As education succeeds in developing man's creative power, we can expect a decrease in mental illness. I believe there is little question that prolonged, enforced repression of a person's creative needs may lead to actual breakdown of personality. Stifling the creative impulse cuts at the very roots of satisfaction in living and ultimately creates overwhelming, paralyzing tension. Man's creativity is his most important weapon in coping with life's daily stresses, its emergencies and crises. In our research we find more and more confirmation of this idea. One set of evidence comes from a study of a group of schizophrenics who were apparently on their way to recovery (Hebeisen, 1959). We were amazed at their tremendous inflexibility, blocking, and lack of imagination. They seemed afraid to think. Clearly, these men and women who had experienced a mental breakdown lacked a most important resource for coping with life's demands. I strongly suspect that this lack explains in large measure why they broke down.

Another consequence of the coming revolution in education will be a considerable decrease in school dropouts at all levels. The student dropout ratio in college is now about 60 per cent (Boroff, 1960). As we learn how to teach more effectively, so that our students are encouraged to use their creative thinking abilities in acquiring knowledge and intellectual skills, a larger number of people will become educable. As we find means of freeing the creative potential of school children, learning and thinking in school will become more exciting and a larger number of able students will be motivated to continue their education. I insist that this will result in a raising of standards. We still maintain that the IQ is a useful metric. Nevertheless, the fact remains that people within a considerable range of IQ's can be educated without any sacrifice of educational standards *when* we teach them in a way that opens up and develops their creative and evaluative thinking abilities.

The nature of education in the kindergarten will also undergo drastic changes. Our work with kindergarteners has shown that they are capable of an excellent quality of creative thought and that they will engage with absorption in creative learning and thinking tasks for longer periods than I had been told was possible. Even now some specialists insist that kindergarten is too much a "holding back" operation, that children at this age have a far greater capacity to learn and think than we now attribute to them, and that present methods impede mental development (Simmons, 1960). No one's potential can be achieved by "holding back" procedures. The limits must be tested!

The traditional differential treatment of boys and girls will also be modified. The creative potentialities of both boys and girls are now being frustrated by misplaced emphases. For years we have been puzzled by the superiority of girls over boys during the early school years and by the superiority of men over women in scientific discovery, invention, musical composition, art, and other high achievement. Our research, however, has already shown that boys excel girls in most of the creative thinking abilities during the second and third grades. If these talents are unrewarded, we can expect boys to resist learning some of the behavioral norms during those years and ultimately to sacrifice their creativity. Girls suffer too. Even though we may not want our girls to be scientific discoverers and inventors, we cannot escape the fact that girls must also adapt to life in the Space Age. Both boys and girls need to talk, ask questions, seek answers, and experiment. I see no need for discriminating between boys and girls in the explanations given about how things work. Girls should be taught to be as accurate and as keen in their observations as boys. Their questions should be taken as seriously as those asked by their brothers. As we make progress in releasing the creative potential of school children, we shall eliminate much of the present social conflict concerning masculine and feminine values. For example, creativity requires both a high degree of sensitivity and a high degree of independence of mind. Sensitivity has a distinctly feminine character in our society; independence, a distinctly masculine character. Thus, the highly creative boy suffers because he appears more effeminate than his peers and the highly creative girl suffers because she appears more masculine than hers.

There are many other possible consequences but I shall mention only one more. As these changes take place in education, school administrators will no longer be able to use the professional literature as a soporific. It has been rumored that many mildly insomniac school administrators and teachers find that ten minutes of reading some of our prominent educational journals is too much for them. After ten minutes of curriculum planning, guidance, or public relations they are sound asleep. The professional literature will be less conducive to somnolence when the exciting changes now taking shape get well underway.

THE CREATIVE CHALLENGE

My final prediction concerns the educator whose duties are administrative. How will he treat the creative challenge? What will he do toward giving the creative potential of his students a chance? This too is fairly predictable. As always, some administrators and supervisors will brush aside the issue and promptly forget about it. Evasion is always a deterrent to adaptation in times of danger and crisis. We resist recognizing the seriousness of the situation and fail to take action.

I hope that more than a few, unable to forget the challenge, will feel they have to do something about it. Some will ask the man on the street and be governed by his opinions. Others will watch the headlines and the school journals; if everyone else is doing it, they will go along. Still others will wait for the perspective of history; the trouble is that in times of increased change and crisis we cannot afford to wait. There are things that can be done now, by those educators who welcome this new charge on their responsibilities.

CONDITIONS FOR CREATIVE GROWTH

THERE is so much talk these days about the need for developing the creative talents of children that the conditions needed for creative growth are sometimes overlooked. By now, I think teachers want to know what they can do to stimulate children to think creatively. First, however, it might be useful to consider a few blunt statements about the importance of creative growth. Here are some of the facts:

1. Although we have long known that it is natural for man to learn creatively, we have almost always insisted that he learn by authority. We now know that many things can be learned creatively by questioning, experimenting, exploring, and testing ideas, and learned more effectively this way than by authority (Torrance, 1962).

2. We now know that children can be taught in ways that bring their creative thinking abilities into use in acquiring even the traditional educational skills (Torrance, 1962), that these abilities are quite different from those measured by our traditional intelligence tests (IQ tests), that these abilities are important to mental or personality health (Hebeisen, 1960), that they are important to vocational success even in such commonplace occupations as department store selling (Wallace, 1961), and that they are important in coping with life's daily stresses.

3. In spite of the importance of these abilities, teachers in general are not appreciably concerned about developing them. This lack of concern is dramatically reflected in statements of the objectives of teachers at all levels of education, in the kinds of activities and assignments teachers initiate, in the kinds of tests and other evaluative procedures of schools, in the methods the schools use to identify talent at all levels from kindergarten through graduate school.

4. It has been demonstrated that the educational concept of over- and under-achievement as gauged from results of intelligence or scholastic aptitude tests is almost completely meaningless (Torrance, 1962). In most schools highly creative children tend to learn as much as children

NOTE: This chapter was originally a paper presented to the elementary and secondary school faculties of the Roseville, Minnesota, public schools, November 14, 1960.

with high IQ's, if we use standardized tests rather than teachers' grades as our criterion.

5. We also know that at all levels of education we do many things that throw the thinking processes off course. In general, however, these abilities tend to grow from kindergarten through third grade, show a marked decrement between the third and fourth grades with recovery in the fifth and sixth grades, drop again between the sixth and seventh, and experience a period of growth from about the eighth to the eleventh grade, at which time there appears to be another period of decline (Torrance, 1962). Some children apparently sacrifice their creativity at about the fourth-grade level and never do regain it.

These facts, together with the unprecedented needs of our society today for creative talent, call for some truly revolutionary changes in educational objectives and in the retooling that must accompany such changes. What is called for is a far cry from the model of the quiz-program champion of a few years ago. Instead of trying to cram a miscellany of facts into the minds of children, making them scientific encyclopedias, we need to ask what kind of children they are becoming. What kind of thinking do they do? How resourceful are they becoming? Are they becoming more responsible? Are they learning to give thoughtful explanations of the things they do and see? Do they believe their own ideas to be of value? Can they share ideas and opinions with others? Do they bring together and relate similar experiences in order to draw conclusions? Do they do some thinking for themselves?

SOCIAL AND CULTURAL CONDITIONS

In our research we have been interested in the factors both in nature and society that affect this growth and in the things that can be manipulated in the classroom. I shall consider first some of the factors in nature that we have found to affect creative development. Afterwards, I shall review briefly ten experiments in which we have manipulated some factor which proved to be significant in stimulating creative thinking of some kind.

These social or cultural conditions first became apparent to us in the course of developing and administering tasks for stimulating creative thinking among children. To the extent possible, we then tried to design studies or reanalyze existing data to obtain confirming evidence.

Success-Orientation. Frequently it has been alleged that we have in the United States a success-oriented culture and that our military and civilian education does not prepare individuals to cope with frustration and failure. Everything detrimental to success must be prevented. As we administered tasks individually to children in the primary grades, the inhibiting effects of their preoccupation with prevention became apparent. The Mother Hubbard problem, for example, asks the subject to think of all of the possible things Mother Hubbard could have done when she found her cupboard bare. We found a growing preoccupation with prevention, reaching perhaps its height in the third grade. When confronted with this problem, third graders tended to give us a blank stare, and say, "What do you mean 'What could she do?'? She shouldn't have let it happen. She should have counted her bones. If she was getting low and didn't have any money, she should have gone to work." They were paralyzed, however, in their consideration of alternative solutions once she was in the predicament.

From a study of mathematics learning among thirteen-year-olds in the Greater Twin Cities area compared with the Greater London area, we have some other interesting data on this issue. We are frequently told that British education does a better job than American education in equipping children to cope with frustration and get themselves out of predicaments. Studies have also shown that British children excel American children in mathematics. One clue from the pilot study, yet to be tested in the full experiment, is the tendency of students in the Greater Twin Cities area to skip the problems with which they have difficulty more frequently than their British counterparts.

The remedy, it seems to me, is to give students more difficult problems — problems they are capable of solving but difficult enough to challenge them, to make them think. In fact, we are not likely to inspire students to do any really creative thinking unless we give them problems of sufficient complexity.

Peer-Orientation. Anthropologists tell us that we have the most peer-oriented culture in the world. Evidence of the inhibiting effects on creative thinking of peer pressures to conformity is too obvious and too widespread to enumerate. We find it when we observe children, when we conduct experiments, when we do sociometric studies, and when we study the creative writing of children. We believe that these phenomena are responsible for the sharp drop in our developmental curves in the fourth grade and again in the seventh. At about the time a child reaches the fourth grade, his need for consensual validation is intensified (Sullivan, 1953). He becomes almost afraid to think until he finds out what his peers are thinking.

This searching for consensual validation is effectively illustrated in the story one father tells of a heated discussion among his children and some of their friends about the sex of their baby rabbits. After much argument about whether these were boy rabbits or girl rabbits, one finally said, "I know how we can tell! Let's vote on it!"

Unusual or original ideas, outstanding performance, and almost any kind of divergent behavior become the target of peer pressures to conformity. This struggle is symbolized in the following story of "The Flying Monkey" by a fifth grader:

"Once there was a little flying monkey who was always doing things his mother told him not to do. One day he was playing outdoors with his little sister and told her, 'I can do something that you cannot do. I can fly!' The little sister said that he could not fly, so he said, 'I will prove it to you.' He went to the end of the branch and began to fly. First he gave a leap and off he went.

"His little sister was so surprised that she ran as fast as she could go to tell the mother monkey. At first the mother monkey did not believe that a monkey could fly. She told the little monkey to go and play and not to bother her. But she finally convinced her mother to come and look. At first she sat and stared and then she told the flying monkey to come back here, but he would not come back. So that night when the father monkey came home, she told him all about it and he went and got the little monkey. He said for him not to fly any more or the other animals would think he was crazy and out of his head."

In many of the stories, the Flying Monkey is lonely, no one will play with him, no one likes him, because he can fly and they can't. It is as plain as that! It is only by some heroic action such as flying the other monkeys to safety when the jungle catches fire that he can win the acceptance of his peers.

Conformity to the peer group is symbolized in a somewhat different way in the story of the "Green Pig," written by a creative fifth grade girl:

"Once upon a time in a far-off land, there was a magic farm that no one has ever visited. Many different animals lived there. The odd thing about these animals was that they were different colors from regular animals.

"The cows were pink, the horses were purple and the hens and chicks were blue! All the pigs were green. That is, all except for one little fellow who was just plain pink. Nobody wanted to be near him or play with him because he wasn't green. And this little pig was very, very sad.

"One day, as he was walking along, he saw a great big puddle of mud. He splashed and rolled in it. When the little pig came out of the puddle, he was all *green*! And he stayed green for the rest of his life. And all of the other pigs began to play with him."

We don't have to look to stories of flying monkeys and green pigs for this kind of material. Perhaps it is more comfortable to do so, in view of the following account in Cedric Adams' column in the *Minneapolis Sunday Tribune* for November 13, 1960:

"There was a student at Henry (High School) named Bill. He was a refugee from Hungary, escaped from there after living 11 years under Communist domination. He had been in America for three years, enrolled at Henry last September. Bill rode his bike to school, a distance of three miles. On his very first day at school he came out to find both tires on his bike slashed well beyond repair. Bullies at the scene told him, 'You're too old to ride a bike to school. You've got to conform — be like the rest of us.' Bill couldn't quite figure it out. This wasn't America the way he knew it. He had his tires replaced. A few days later he found his tires slashed and the wheels on his bike twisted completely out of shape . . ."

Apparently Bill hadn't heard about the tyranny of the peer culture in America. He lacked the wisdom of the authors of our stories about green pigs and flying monkeys.

We hope that in time we shall learn more about this problem from studying the development of the creative thinking abilities in other cultures outside the United States and in some special subcultures within this country. We believe that teachers and parents can create a climate that will permit a healthy type of individualism, of divergent thinking. Certainly, some conformities are essential, but perhaps we too often require conformity where divergency would be preferable.

Someone has observed that almost always wherever independence and creativity occur and persist, there is **found** some person or agent who plays the role of "sponsor" or "patron." The sponsor or patron is not a member of the peer group, but possesses prestige or power in the same social system. Regardless of his own views, the sponsor encourages and supports the creative person in expressing and testing his ideas, in thinking through things for himself. The sponsor protects him from the counterreactions of his peers long enough to permit him to try out some of his ideas, keeping the structure of the situation open long enough so that originality *can* occur. In some cases, this sponsor for a child may be a teacher, a principal, an older child, an adult leader in a youth organization, or the like.

I know of a principal who is performing this function for a highly creative fourth grade boy. During an experiment conducted at her school I observed the outstanding creative talent of this youngster. In the classroom, I had described the small-group task that was set up to discover unusual applications of science toys and to explain the underlying scientific principles. On the way to the room where his group was to meet, he remarked that he hoped the task would offer something to which he could apply Newton's Third Law of Motion. His performance in the experiment was so remarkable that I mentioned it casually to the principal afterwards. A few days later we returned to this school to conduct the same experiment in other classes. In the meantime, the principal had visited this boy's mathematics class, during which the boy questioned one of the rules in the book. Instead of asking him to prove his interpretation or trying to explain the textbook rule herself, the teacher became quite irritated, even in the presence of the principal. Holding up the book and patting it with the other hand, she exclaimed, "So! You think you know more than this book!" The boy replied meekly, "No, I don't think I know more than the book, but I'm not satisfied about this rule." Moving to safer ground, the teacher then had the class solve problems in the text. This youngster solved the problems easily, about as rapidly as he could read them, thereby upsetting his teacher, who insisted that he put down all the steps he had gone through in solving the problems. Afterwards, the teacher asked the principal to talk to her troublesome pupil. The principal explained to the boy that many things "came easy" to him, such as solving the problems without writing down all the steps. She also explained that there were some skills, like handwriting, which came easier to others than to him, and that he might have to work harder than others on these skills. Apparently, she has played this role of sponsorship for this boy for two or three years.

Sanctions against Questioning and Exploration. Although we generally recognize the need for children to ask questions and in other ways inquire about the wonders and mysteries of their world, we still do a brutal job of squelching such tendencies. We have perfected many devices of ridicule and evasion for putting the curious child in his place. We usually tell him that "curiosity killed the cat." It has been my observation, however, that cats are highly skilled in calculating risks and soon learn what they are capable of doing, while most children are never given the chance to realize their capabilities. I have also observed that curious people are never idle.

This exploring, inquiring kind of behavior so important to creativity begins before the child's first words are uttered. A baby handles things, shakes, twists, and turns them upside down, and I believe these infantile manipulations are forerunners of the process which may later lead to creative work in science, art, or some other field. In our own laboratory experiments we find a significant relationship between degree of manipulation and quantity and quality of inventive response. To develop creative thinking, it is important to permit and encourage children to manipulate, to play with objects, words, and ideas, to the extent possible within the limits of safety. There is much that we as educators can do to arrange the conditions so that occasional failure at tasks is not permitted to threaten or inhibit creativity. Some interesting work is also being done on training children in skills of questioning and inquiry.

Overemphasis or Misplaced Emphasis on Sex Roles. That boys excel girls, and girls boys, in different kinds of creative activity has been one of the most consistent findings about creative thinking during the past sixty or seventy years (Torrance, 1962). Almost always these differences can be explained on the basis of the contrasting roles that our culture imposes on boys and girls. It has been pointed out frequently that women rarely become scientific discoverers, inventors, or composers. Overemphasis or misplaced emphasis on sex roles, however, exacts its toll on the creativity of both sexes and burdens the exceptional child with serious problems of adjustment.

Creativity, by its very nature, requires both sensitivity and independence. In our culture, sensitivity is definitely a feminine virtue, while independence is a masculine value. Thus, we may expect the highly creative boy to appear more effeminate than his peers and the highly creative girl more masculine than hers. Roe (1959), Barron (1957), and I (see pp. 152–158) have all cited evidence in support of this phenomenon. In our longitudinal studies we are finding interesting examples of children who sacrifice their creativity in order to maintain their "masculinity" or their "femininity," as the case may be.

This cultural block to creativity comes out in many places. We first observed it in our Product Improvement Test, in which children are asked to think of all the ideas they can for improving common toys so that they will be more fun to play with (Torrance and Bowers, 1959). In the first grade, boys excelled girls on the fire truck but girls excelled boys on the nurse's kit. Many of the boys refused to think of anything to make the nurse's kit more fun, protesting, "I'm a boy! I don't play with things like that!" Some of the more creative boys, however, first transposed it into a doctor's kit and only then felt quite free to think of improvements. By the third grade, however, boys excelled girls even on the nurse's kit, probably because by this time girls have been conditioned to accept toys as they are and not to manipulate and change them.

The inhibiting effects of sex-role conditioning also showed up in our experiments involving small groups working with science toys (see pp.

119–136). Girls are quite reluctant to work with these science toys and frequently protest that the toys are not appropriate for girls. Boys demonstrate and explain about twice as many ideas as girls in experiments involving these materials. We know already, however, that this situation can be modified significantly (see pp. 145–151). In 1959 we found these phenomena operating quite strongly in the school where these experiments were conducted. Later I had the opportunity to report these and other results to both the teachers and the parents in this school. In 1960 we conducted some experiments in this same school, in which we used a different but similar set of science toys. This time, we found none of this reluctance on the part of girls; there was no difference in the expressed enjoyment of the activity of boys and girls; the mean performance of boys and girls was almost identical. In one way, however, the situation remained unchanged. The contributions of boys were more highly valued by peers than those of girls. Apparently, the school climate had helped to make it more acceptable for girls to play with science things, but boys' ideas about science things were still supposed to be better than those of girls.

The social consequences of failure to achieve the behavioral norms associated with sex roles are well understood by children by the time they reach the fourth grade, if not before. Such an understanding is reflected in the following story of "The Lion That Doesn't Roar":

"Our story begins in the Belgian Congo where we came upon a den of lions. The mother had just had babies. The father was very proud and wanted to make them kings of the jungle. When they were still young, they had a contest to see who could roar the loudest.

"First, Tarzan tried and first a cough and then a choke and then a little roar. More of a purr, really though. Next was Leo, Jr., a fine example of his father. He cleared his throat, then a deep breath and a gigantic roar for his age. Third and last, Ollie, a little tyke and not much of a lion. He tried and tried but all he could do was purr.

"Father was proud of Leo and fairly proud of Tarzan. But Ollie was a flop in his eyes."

The story also illustrates the difficulty we encounter when we use a single criterion of giftedness, or overemphasize only one kind of giftedness — whether it be IQ, creativity, athletic ability, or whatever.

Divergency Equated with Abnormality. Once even leading thinkers believed "genius" and "madness" to be closely associated. Almost all inventors, composers, creative scientists, and other eminent men were regarded as more or less insane. Although these notions were discredited long ago, somehow the belief has persisted that any divergence from behavioral norms is an indication of the abnormal, or the unhealthy, and is to be corrected at all costs. In spite of definitions of the truly healthy personality as being different both from the "normal" or "average" personality and from the unhealthy, and in spite of theories of psychotherapy which stress self-fulfillment and creative living, divergence from the norm is still regarded with suspicion.

From the imaginative stories composed by children, I gather that children are taught very early that divergent characteristics or behavior are signs of mental illness, as in the story already cited of the flying monkey whose father pled with him not to fly because others would think he was "crazy." The following story of "The Cat That Wouldn't Scratch" suggests some different aspects of the problem:

"Once there was a cat that would not scratch. A lady came and the cat was following her so she took the cat home with her. The cat meowed and meowed, so the lady gave him some milk. She noticed that the cat was dirty because he hadn't had anybody to care for him. So the lady put the cat in the bath tub and gave him a bath but he did not scratch her. The lady did not understand. She had never seen a cat that wouldn't scratch when you gave him a bath. So she took the cat to the cat hospital. They did not understand so she let him go and that is the end of the cat that would not scratch and the lady and the doctor that did not understand the cat."

To some children the pressures of society to rid them of divergent characteristics appear to be relentless, as vividly illustrated in the story of "The Duck That Couldn't Quack":

"Quack! Quack! They were after him again — the Ladies Duck Aid Society, with their hair up in pin curls and their screaming, fat ducklings swimming and holding onto their skirts. They never failed. Alas! It was getting to be too much for little Glob-Blob. Every day there would be flying of feathers and screaming of ducklings while poor Glob-Blob would run as fast as he could to get away from these vicious ducks. The reason for this was because Glob-Blob could not quack. So every day the Ladies Duck Aid Society would chase Glob-Blob, for they said it was for the good of the ducks and it was not only right but they were doing a good turn.

"It was lucky for Glob-Blob that the ducks were fat and flabby, for if they were limber, I will not mention what would happen. But one day, these lazy ducks did reduce and dealt Glob-Blob a good many heavy blows. And the next day, poor Glob-Blob was at last doomed. The vicious quackers came and the chase was on. Glob-Blob was failing. It is a shame that so noble a duck should be doomed, but "That is life," said

Glob-Blob to himself as, slowly but surely, failing, he dropped to the ground. The quackers, very pleased with themselves, sat down for a chat.

"But I shall always remember Glob-Blob and his death. So I shall leave him now and let him continue his journey where there will be no more quackers and chasers, and where at last, he may have passionless peace forever."

I wonder if we would do well sometimes to ask ourselves if we are "quackers and chasers" when we work so hard to turn children into "better rounded personalities." They might contribute far more to society and be far happier if allowed to capitalize upon their unique strengths rather than spend fruitless energy in trying hopelessly to compensate for so-called weakness. I would not, of course, deny that it is necessary for the highly creative youngster to acquire any neglected basic skills that might be necessary for success in his chosen area of specialization.

Work-Play Dichotomy. Another characteristic of our culture which serves to block creative development is our work-play dichotomy. The child is supposed to enjoy play and is considered peculiar if he doesn't. He is supposed to dislike work, and is considered abnormal if he doesn't. I think the distinction between work and play is one of the main reasons why more teachers don't give children more opportunities to learn creatively. What the children enjoy makes the teachers uneasy. School is supposed to be work, not fun. In those schools with an austere, no-fun atmosphere I find the least evidence that the creative thinking abilities are used in learning. There is a real need for more "mental sunshine" in many classrooms.

We ought to recognize that perhaps the greatest reward for learning is thinking — doing something with what has been learned. We do find that children enjoy performing our tests of creative thinking ability. One kindergarten class is reported to have greeted their teacher when she returned the day after our testing with: "Gee, you ought to have been here yesterday. That man sure did work us hard, but gee was it fun!" A fourth grade class didn't want to be interrupted when the recess bell rang and protested, "Don't make us stop. This is more fun than recess, anyway!"

Another interesting clue comes from our study differentiating highly intelligent from highly creative children, described in the preceding paper. There was a difference of 25 IQ points between these two groups (the upper 20 per cent in the group on these two measures) but no difference in their measured achievement. Ordinarily we would have to say either that the highly creatives are over-achieving or that the high IQ group is under-achieving. The teachers, however, rated the high creatives as less ambitious and hard-working. Yet with IQ's averaging 25 points lower, and being less ambitious and hard-working, they still learned as much as their more intelligent classmates. Apparently they had been learning through activities that appeared to adults as idle play. Apparently this seemingly purposeless activity is one of their ways of learning.

I was also interested in the reactions of some of the teachers in our creative writing experiments. In drawing up a list of suggested titles, since we were anxious to think of titles that would spark the imagination of the children, be new to them, permit them to regress, and bring out their concepts about divergent characteristics and behavior, we picked topics like the following: "The Flying Monkey"; "The Lion That Won't Roar"; "The Cat That Won't Scratch"; "The Woman Who Won't Talk"; "The Man Who Cries." Some teachers objected that these subjects were not suitable for boys and girls to write about, because they were silly and unrealistic. They also objected to our de-emphasis on correct spelling, good handwriting, and general mechanics.

I realize that it will be some time before our understanding of the creative process will make it possible for teachers to discard some of their rigidity and constriction and accept the conditions necessary for what Maslow (1962) calls "primary creativeness." By this is meant the kind of creativity that "comes out of the preconscious; is the source of discovery and ideas which depart from what exists at the moment; is common and universal to all people; is found in healthy children; comes from those who are able to play, fantasy, and laugh; and comes from those who accept their softness and femininity and some weaknesses in themselves."

Thus far, I have discussed those conditions affecting creativity which became apparent — even obvious — as we attempted to study them and to conduct experiments. In describing some of these conditions we have cited research evidence. At best, however, nature conducted these experiments for us. Now, I should like to review in the barest detail the results of ten experiments in which we manipulated and assessed the effects of one or more variables.

EXPERIMENTALLY MANIPULATED CONDITIONS

Although a variety of materials has been used in our experiments, the basic design for most has been the same throughout. Groups have been divided by some random procedure for the types of experimental training under study and the training period has been followed by a task requiring some type or types of creative thinking. In most of the experiments results have been analyzed separately for each grade, generally from grades one through six, and totaling around four hundred subjects in each experiment.

Training in Principles. In one of our earliest experiments we tried to determine whether we could train children during a twenty-minute period to apply a set of principles and thereby increase the quantity and quality of their ideas (see pp. 137–144). We used the principles developed by Osborn and his associates: making the object larger, making the object smaller, rearrangement, combination, adapting, changing color, giving motion, giving odor, changing shape, giving sound, and the like. In the experimental condition, practice was given in thinking of ideas to improve a toy fire truck, to make it more fun to play with, and was followed by training in generalization based on a square — which had been "improved" by all these methods — and on the establishment of connections between the "square model" and improvements on the fire truck. The test task involved thinking of ideas for improving a toy stuffed dog.

In all grades there was a consistent tendency for the trained subjects to produce more responses, more flexible records, and more clever or original responses than the untrained ones. The differences in the first and fifth grades, however, did not reach statistical significance, except for greater flexibility in the fifth grade.

It was concluded that pupils in the early school years, with the possible exception of the first and fifth grades, can be taught a set of principles in a short time that will enable them to achieve greater flexibility of ideation and produce a larger number of clever or original ideas as well as a larger total number of ideas. Longer and/or spaced periods of training would probably produce more conclusive results.

Motivation for Quantity vs. Quality. Using the same experimental set-up described above, one group was motivated for quantity (think of as many ideas as you can; don't worry about how good they are) and the other for quality (think of the cleverest, most interesting, and most unusual ideas you can).

In the first three grades there was a consistent trend for the motivation to produce "clever, interesting, and unusual" ideas to be more effective than the motivation for quantity regardless of quality. There was a consistent trend in the opposite direction in the fourth, fifth, and sixth grades. Acceptable levels of statistical significance were achieved only in the second and fourth grades, however. Although these findings are not very convincing, Osborn's principle of motivation for quantity without regard for quality appears to be inappropriate for use in the first three grades. It may have some value, however, at about the third grade.

Competition. The same general experimental set-up described above was used to study the effects of competition. Under competitive conditions a prize was offered for the children in each grade who thought of the most and "best" ideas. Under noncompetitive conditions, no prize was offered.

At every grade level, children under competitive conditions produced a larger number of ideas, showed greater flexibility, and produced more clever ideas. At all levels the differences were statistically significant.

In a second experiment (Torrance and Krishnaiah, 1960), competition was pitted against a "warm-up" experience in which children practiced on the fire truck before being asked to think of ideas for improving the toy dog. There was still a fairly consistent tendency for children under competitive conditions to excel those under the "warm-up" conditions. Results were statistically significant in only the first (fluency), second (flexibility), third (fluency and flexibility), and fourth grades (fluency and flexibility). Thus, it appears that children above the fourth grade may be as responsive to some kinds of "warm-up" experience as to competition. It was also concluded that a "warm-up" experience at least in part compensates for lack of competition in the first four grades.

Unevaluated vs. Evaluated Practice. In another set of experiments (Schenitzki, 1961) using the Shape Picture Completion and Incomplete Figures tasks, we experimented with unevaluated and evaluated practice. In the first condition, the children were urged to experiment, to try out various things, not to be afraid of messing up their materials, and the like. They were assured that the practice would not count toward their winning the prize on the test task later. Under the evaluated condition, the children were given helpful suggestions during and following the practice session and no assurance was given that the practice work was "off the record." The instructions were designed to encourage two types of creative thinking: originality and elaboration. The products were evaluated for these and other creative qualities.

In general, the unevaluated practice was more effective than evaluated practice in encouraging creativity in the first three grades but not in the upper grades. On one task (the Shape task), however, unevaluated practice was also more effective in the fourth grade. In the first grade the evaluated condition produced greater originality than unevaluated practice.

On the basis of these findings, it may be concluded that, generally speaking, children in the primary grades will respond favorably to un-evaluated practice or freedom from immediate evaluation. We had observed previously that timid children in the primary grades responded favorably in the individual testing situation when urged "to do it just for fun, that it didn't count."

It is impossible to say what would happen in the upper grades, if unevaluated practice were continued. Responses in the present experiment might have been conditioned by the children's prior experience in being evaluated all of the time. They may have been skeptical about the experimenter's assurances.

Critical and Creative Peer Evaluation. In an experiment to assess the effects of critical and creative peer evaluation (Schenitzki, 1961), the same experimental set-up described above was used. In the Critical Peer Evaluation condition the children were asked to criticize one another's work following each practice exercise. Emphasis was placed on defects or faults. In the Creative Peer Evaluation condition, the children were asked to suggest improvements for making each other's products more interesting, more unusual, or to add other ideas about the products.

From kindergarten through third grade, no statistically significant differences occurred on either of the two tasks. Most of the differences were statistically significant, however, in the fourth, fifth, and sixth grades. We think these results indicate that children in the kindergarten and primary grades are not bothered by the opinions of their peers but that negative criticism in the fourth, fifth, and sixth grades puts a damper on creative thinking.

Creativity Training and Improvement of Creative Writing. In an experiment conducted by R. E. Myers (1960), a random half of the children in a class were given intensive training in creative thinking over a period of four months but no training in creative writing. The other half were given training in convergent problem solving. As measured by pre- and post-tests of creative writing, the children who had been given creativity training showed greater growth than their controls.

In an experiment in Minneapolis and St. Paul, we urged a group of teachers to try out a number of ideas for developing creative thinking through language-arts activities. Although our controls reported using as many of these ideas as the experimentals, we obtained some interesting results. When these teachers were split at the median on the number of ideas tried, and when the performances of their pupils were then compared, we obtained significant results. The pupils of the teachers who reported using the largest number of creative activities showed significant growth in creative writing over a three-month period, whereas no growth was found for the pupils of those teachers in the lower half on number of activities tried. The evidence for the transfer effects of creativity training on creative writing therefore appears promising.

Homogeneous and Heterogeneous Groupings. Fourth, fifth, and sixth grade classes in three schools were divided into five-person groups (Torrance and Arsan, 1961). Some classes were divided homogeneously and some heterogeneously, in two schools on the basis of creativity and in the third on the basis of IQ. Each group was given the Science-Toy task already mentioned. During the initial twenty-five-minute period, the group was instructed to experiment and try to discover as many uses, intended and unintended, of the toys as possible and to demonstrate and explain as many scientific principles as possible. The second twenty-five-minute period was devoted to the demonstrations and explanations.

When the groups were divided heterogeneously on the basis of creativity, there was a strong tendency for the more creative members to initiate the most ideas and to demonstrate and explain the most principles. The tendency was a linear one. No such linear tendency was observed when the basis of heterogeneity was IQ. In fact, the low IQ children tended to do as well as the high IQ ones. In the homogeneous conditions, the low groups tended to go all out and excel or equal the high groups. In general, the groups at the third and fourth levels of ability tended to perform most poorly.

In this same experimental set-up (Torrance, 1961b) we were also interested in studying the problem of social stress in homogeneous and heterogeneous groups within classes for creative activities. Observers' records were carefully analyzed for signs of social stress and signs of positive, productive interaction.

The following terms were counted as indications of disruptive social stress: bickering, fighting, squabbling, uncontrolled behavior, disorder, disorganization, domination, squelching, reprimanding, loss of temper, apathy, refusal to cooperate, loss of interest, sarcasm, disruptive talking and joking.

The following were considered signs of positive, productive interaction: cooperating, helping, working together, organizing, absorption in task, praising one another, respecting others' ideas, listening, considering others' ideas, trying out others' ideas, communicating ideas, consulting with one another, congenial, interested, questioning, curious.

The results revealed significantly more signs of social stress in the heterogeneous than in the homogeneous groups in all three schools. We concluded that teachers, by their choice of homogeneous or heterogeneous groupings within a class, may influence the degree of social stress in groups working on creative tasks. At times, heterogeneous groups may be desirable; in other situations, homogeneous groups may be more effective.

In the heterogeneous groups formed on the basis of creativity tests, a number of interesting findings resulted from an analysis of the pressures exerted by the group on the most creative member and the counterstrategies adopted by the creative.

In one school, the experiment was extended downward to the second grade (see pp. 119–136). From second through sixth grade a decreasing tendency for group members to work alone, especially the most creative ones, rather than as a part of a group, was revealed. The tendency for the most creative children to work alone persists fairly strongly through the fifth grade, at which point the tendency for groups to organize begins to emerge as an important technique of control. Techniques for controlling the most creative member include: open aggression and hostility, criticism, rejection and/or indifference, the use of organizational machinery to limit scope of operation and to impose sanctions, exaltation to a position of power involving excessive paper work and administrative responsibility, and the like. Adaptation techniques of the most creative members include: compliance, counteraggressiveness, indomitable persistence, apparent ignoring of criticism, clowning, silence and apathy or preoccupation, inconsistent performance, filling the gaps when others falter, solitary activity, and the like.

The "Idea Trap." The "idea-trap" plan promoted by Osborn (1957), Clark (1958), and others was applied to the creative writing activities in one school from grade three through six (Hiller, 1961). Using a weekly magazine, named by the children "Ideas of the Week," as a motivating device, children were encouraged to write on their own. In the demonstration experiment, it was found that most children (over 90 per cent) responded favorably to this plan, generating much enthusiasm and developing increased appreciation of the value of their own ideas and those of their classmates.

Rewarding Creative Thinking. We know through research that children and adults learn and develop along whatever lines they find rewarding. For the use of teachers, a manual entitled *Rewarding Creative Thinking* was developed by the author and his colleagues. The following six principles from this manual were also used in an in-service training program in a field experiment: (1) Treat questions with respect. (2)

Treat imaginative, unusual ideas with respect. (3) Show pupils that their ideas have value. (4) Give opportunities for practice or experimentation without evaluation. (5) Encourage and evaluate self-initiated learning. (6) Tie in evaluation with causes and consequences.

Users of the manual are asked to describe and evaluate specific attempts of their own in applying these principles. Many teachers respond favorably to workshop experiences and to suggestions provided by manuals. Skillful application of these principles appears to lead to creative growth.

Creative Attitudes of Teachers. Teachers participating in the creative writing experiments were administered the Personal-Social Motivation Inventory, which yields a score defined as "Creative Attitude." Participating teachers were divided at the median into a "high creative" and a "low creative group." We found that the high creatives tried out a larger number of the ideas included in the manual entitled "A Collection of Ideas for Developing the Creative Thinking Abilities through the Language Arts." Their pupils showed significant growth in creative writing, whereas the pupils of those teachers in the lower half actually showed a slight decrement between the pre- and post-test of creative writing.

Teachers as Hypothesis Makers. We have also become interested in the ability of the teacher as a hypothesis maker, an ability important to our concept of creative teaching. Recently we obtained some interesting data on the hypothesis-making behavior of teachers in connection with experimental mathematics courses being conducted in a number of Minnesota schools (Torrance, 1961c). First, we analyzed the daily logs of the most and least effective teachers. Compared with the least effective teachers, the most effective reported far more thinking activities for themselves and their pupils. This included all kinds of problem-solving, creative thinking, questioning, inquiry, evaluation, and the like. A comparison of the logs of the most and least effective teachers in 1959–60 revealed almost the same picture. Then a detailed analysis of the evaluative thinking of these teachers showed that the least effective of these mathematics teachers reported more praise or positive evaluation as well as more negative criticism than the more effective ones. The more effective teachers reported far more troubleshooting or hypothesis-making behavior than their less effective colleagues. They consistently tried to put their finger on any difficulties they sensed or experienced in their teaching, and they advanced hypotheses concerning the cause and nature of any such difficulty — say, in their relations with a student — and freely speculated about possible remedies.

RESEARCH AT OTHER LEVELS

I have not discussed here our experiments conducted at the graduate level because of our primary concern in this report with the conditions for creativity in the early school years. In time, we expect that many of our findings about adults may prove to be adaptable for use with children and adolescents. From the differences already found between the primary and intermediate grades, however, it is clear that such findings need to be thoroughly tested at all educational levels.

MENTAL HEALTH PROBLEMS OF HIGHLY CREATIVE CHILDREN

In this paper I shall sketch eight typical situations, or verbal pictures, from our Minnesota Studies of Creative Thinking, which provide information on the mental health problems of highly creative school children. Then I shall propose a general conceptualization for investigating these problems and applying the results.

SOCIOMETRIC POSITION OF A CREATIVE CHILD

My first picture is of the sociometric position of a highly creative boy in a class of thirty-five third graders in a public school. I shall call this boy Jim. On our tests of creative thinking, he displayed some of the most inventive, original, and flexible behavior we have found in testing several thousand children. Jim's Stanford-Binet IQ was 135. In spite of these intellectual talents, Jim was one of the school's most serious problems. He was not learning to read, had become a behavior problem, and frequently became so preoccupied with his thoughts that he didn't know what was going on in class.

Figure 1 shows the peer nominations received by the six most creative children in Jim's class on the criterion, "Who in your class thinks of a lot of good ideas?" Jim, we see, received no nominations in spite of his outstanding ability to produce good ideas. When we ask, "Who in your class thinks of a lot of wild or silly ideas?" we see that Jim is a real star here (Figure 2). We obtain the same picture when we ask, "Who thinks of a lot of ideas for being naughty?"

Other clues emerge when we examine Jim's productions on the House-Tree-Person Test. His house is neatly drawn but has no windows or doors, except for a tiny window high in the attic, suggesting a high degree of psychological inaccessibility. His tree and person are quite unusual and cannot be evaluated very easily by the criteria developed by Buck (1948), Goodenough (1949), Machover (1948), or anyone else.

Note: This chapter was originally a paper presented at the annual meeting of the American Psychological Association, New York, August 31, 1961.

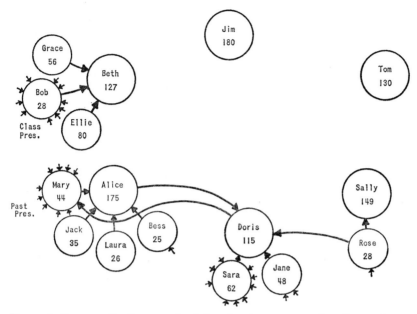

Figure 1. Peer nominations received by the six most creative (large circles) among thirty-five third graders on the criterion "Who in the class thinks of the best good ideas?" (Number of ideas produced on test appears below each name. Each arrow indicates a nomination.)

TEST PERFORMANCE OF SCHIZOPHRENICS

Let us turn now from Jim's struggle between maintaining or sacrificing his creativity and the resulting problems of uncertain self-concepts, learning difficulties, delinquency, and moments of schizophrenic-like withdrawal. The picture I want to present is the one we obtain from the performance on a battery of creative thinking tasks of a sample of seventy-one schizophrenic patients, apparently on the road to recovery, with most of them under consideration for vocational rehabilitation.

The picture is a stark one of impoverished imagination and frozen creativity — amazing inflexibility, banality, blocking, and clinging to the safe and obvious. Their lack of flexibility is strikingly illustrated by the scoring of a task calling for them to think of as many interesting and unusual uses of tin cans as they could. Eighty-seven per cent of their responses are the obvious container uses (Figure 3). In contrast, 33 per cent of the college sophomore and junior responses and 17 per cent of the fourth, fifth, and sixth grade responses were of this type. Their inability to summon creative responses of any kind is reflected in

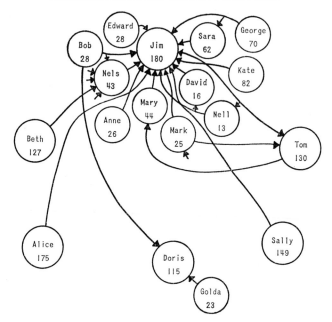

Figure 2. Peer nominations received by the six most creative among thirty-five third graders on the criterion "Who in the class thinks of the most silly or wild ideas?"

the data presented in Figure 4. About 60 per cent of the schizophrenic group blocked completely on four or more of the thirteen tasks; none of the college or elementary school subjects blocked on this many.

Is there any relationship between the struggles of our highly creative third grader and the performance of the schizophrenic subjects on tests of creative thinking? In the following six situations or pictures, I shall present some findings which may help us piece together or project some intelligent guesses about the missing links.

PERSONALITIES OF HIGHLY CREATIVE CHILDREN

A part of this picture unfolds when we compare the personality data of the most creative boy and girl in each of twenty-three elementary classrooms, with children matched carefully for IQ, sex, age, teacher, and race. Three differentiating characteristics stand out. First, the highly creative children far more frequently have reputations for having wild or silly ideas. Second, their productions, whatever their nature, tend to be off the beaten track. Third, their work is characterized by humor and playfulness.

Schizophrenic Group

College Sophomores
and Juniors

Fourth, Fifth, and
Sixth Grade Pupils

Figure 3. Percentages of container responses given by three samples asked to suggest unusual uses of tin cans.

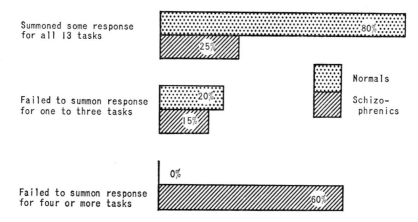

Summoned some response
for all 13 tasks

Failed to summon response
for one to three tasks

Failed to summon response
for four or more tasks

Figure 4. Percentage of normals (college sophomores and juniors) showing various degrees of blocking on a battery of thirteen creative thinking tasks.

A glimpse of another part of the picture is given by the "blind analyses" of the data from the House-Tree-Person drawings. The following sketch of a fourth-grade boy will serve as an illustration:

"This fourth-grade boy is rather inaccessible psychologically. He is likely to be defensive in his social relations and the area of satisfaction from his environment is quite constricted. There is little place for fantasy in his environment and there are many constraints against his reaching out and exploring his environment. He seeks satisfaction through intellectual effort and delays emotional satisfaction. He is experiencing feelings of weakness and futility in interpersonal relationships. He is likely to be quite sensitive to criticism and bothered by feelings of inferiority."

Many of these studies suggest that the rejection of certain personality trends by peers and teachers seems to threaten the creative promise of the talented children. I would not place a great deal of weight on this third picture, if it were not reinforced quite strongly by the remaining three.

TEACHERS' PORTRAITS OF CREATIVE CHILDREN

The descriptive portraits of highly creative children painted by their teachers significantly illustrate teachers' attitudes of rejection. When highly creative children are contrasted with highly intelligent children, following the Getzels-Jackson (1962) design, we discover that teachers do not "know" them as well, regard them as less desirable pupils, rate them as less ambitious and hard-working, and nominate them far more frequently as having wild or silly ideas. Ratings on the "good-ideas" criterion seem to be determined by the proportion of "good" ideas to total number of ideas produced rather than by the number of "good" ideas produced. In describing their ideal pupil, teachers tend to reject many of the characteristics of highly creative individuals.

INHIBITING EFFECTS OF SEX STEREOTYPES

This picture, based in part on the use of different kinds of toys in our product improvement task, is highlighted in the results from first graders. When asked how they would make the toys "more fun to play with,"

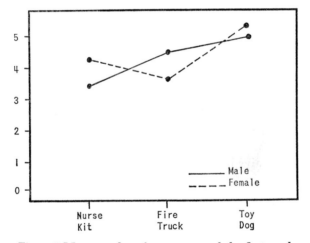

Figure 5. Mean number of responses made by first grade boys and first grade girls on each of three toy-improvement tasks.

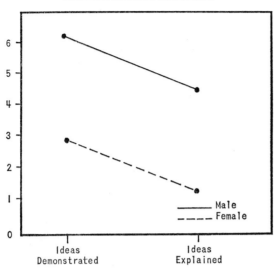

Figure 6. Mean number of ideas demonstrated and explained by boys and girls on the science-toy task.

boys suggested more ideas for improving a toy fire truck and fewer for improving a nurse's kit. The results, shown in Figure 5, would have been more dramatic had some of our more creative boys not first transformed the nurse's kit into a doctor's kit, thus making it appropriate for boys, and therefore acceptable to them.

Another part of the picture unfolds in the behavior of girls confronted with science toys in an experiment. Many of the girls expressed dislike for the task, saying, "I'm a girl; I'm not supposed to know anything about things like that." As shown in Figure 6, boys demonstrated and explained twice as many ideas as girls. These and other data suggest that the pressures of sex-role expectations block off certain areas of thinking among both sexes.

OBSERVED PEER PRESSURES

This picture emerges from an experimental study of the pressures exerted by small groups on their most creative members, to hold them in check. In each five-person group in a class, we placed one of the most creative children (as identified by a battery of creative thinking tasks). The competitive group task was to discover as many uses, intended and unintended, as possible for a collection of science toys. In each of thirty-seven such groups from grades two through six, pressures to hold in check the most creative member were clearly indicated. Sixty-eight per cent of the most creative members initiated and explained more ideas than any other member of the group. In only 24 per cent of the groups were these members rated by their peers as contributing most to the group's success.

The behavior of these highly creative children is in interesting contrast to that reported by Merei (1949) for children gifted in leadership ability. When introduced into already functioning groups, Merei's little "leadership types" gained control by first accepting the group's traditions and ways of doing things. Few of our highly creative subjects displayed either the willingness to accept the group's way of doing things or the desire to control the group.

Techniques of control employed against the most creative group members included: open aggression and hostility, negative criticism, rejection and/or indifference, use of organizational machinery to limit scope of operation and to impose sanctions, and reducing opportunity by assigning paperwork or administrative responsibility. Adaptation techniques of the highly creative children included: compliance, counteraggressiveness, indomitable persistence, apparent ignoring of criticism, clowning, silence and apathy or preoccupation, inconsistent performance, solitary activity, and filling the gaps when the others falter.

CHILDREN'S PERCEPTIONS OF DIVERGENCY

To gain information about the perceptions of children concerning divergency and society's handling of divergent behavior, we have collected several thousand imaginative stories from children from grades three through nine, concerning animals and persons with some kind of divergent characteristic, such as flying monkeys, lions that won't roar, girls who want to be engineers, and boys who want to be nurses.

The pressures of society against divergency are recognized by children as powerful forces, but there are considerable variations among cultures. Perhaps the most severe pressures against creative kinds of achievement, and toward the formation of well-rounded personalities, are found in the stories from heterogeneous classes in urban areas. Gifted children in special classes are far more optimistic about chances of persisting in creative, divergent behavior than gifted children in regular classes. Stories written by children in small towns reflect far more tolerance of divergence than those of urban children. Stories written by children in a small Oklahoma town (consisting of American Indians, whites, and a few Negroes) reflect the highest degree of tolerance of creative, divergent behavior of any group thus far. The stories of children in schools controlled by religious bodies reflect the greatest intolerance.

The stories of Negro children in a segregated school in Georgia reflect the greatest parental support of divergent talent.

Of several cultures outside the United States, the stories of French children reflect perhaps the highest tolerance of divergency and those of Greek children the greatest interest in trying to understand and explain divergent behavior.

DEVELOPMENTAL CURVES FOR CREATIVE THINKING

Although there are slight variations for different tasks and factors, the pattern of developmental curves is remarkably consistent from culture to culture, from one period of history to another, and from investigator to investigator. The developmental curve shown in Figure 7 may be regarded as a generalized one and holds for most of the tasks and factors for samples taken within the United States. As nearly as I can establish it from work such as that of Andrews (1930), a peak is reached at about age four and a half, followed by a decline at about age five. In our studies, we have found that as the child adapts to school a period of growth occurs in the first through the third grades. A rather sharp slump near the end of the third or beginning of the fourth is followed by another period of growth in the fifth and sixth. Entrance into junior high school is accompanied by another drop. Again recovery and growth resume until near the end of the high school period, at which time there is a slight slump or leveling off.

It is quite possible that many of the problems of mental health are related to these critical slump periods, especially the one in the fourth grade. In our Australian sample, this slump occurs in the fifth grade and in Western Samoa, the third. Children in Australia are slightly younger and in Western Samoa slightly older for their grade than in the United States.

A TENTATIVE CONCEPTUALIZATION

All of these and many other threads of evidence have suggested to me a general conceptualization for investigating and ameliorating the problems of highly creative individuals. Such a framework can be sketched here only in the barest outline.

Since almost all definitions of creativity involve the production of something new, original, or divergent, we must begin with the inescapable fact that any person who thinks of a new idea is in the beginning a minority of one. Even when matters of fact are involved, as in the Asch (1955) experiments, there are few people who can endure being a minority of one, which leaves a person with too few "anchors in reality."

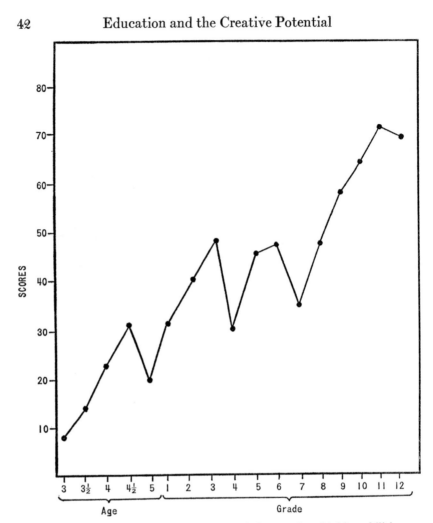

Figure 7. Generalized developmental curve of the creative thinking abilities.

Since creativity requires independence of mind, divergence from group norms, or unusualness, it is inevitable that highly creative persons will experience many problems of adjustment. The highly creative child must either repress or sacrifice his creativity or learn to cope with or reduce the tensions that arise from being so frequently a minority of one. Such regression, if prolonged or severe, leads to uncertain or inadequate self-concepts, learning difficulties, behavior problems, neurotic distortions, or even psychotic breakdowns. The continued expression of creative needs in spite of tensions and pressures, however, may lead to loneliness, conflicts, or other types of reduced contact with the environment.

In trying to piece together the missing links between the initial picture of Jim, the highly creative third-grade boy and the test performance of the sample of schizophrenic subjects, we cannot say to what extent a breakdown occurred because the subject sacrificed his creativity. As our longitudinal studies progress, we hope to gain further useful information concerning this issue. Meanwhile, my own hypothesis is that the roots of the difficulty stem from the inevitable pressures that are exerted against the expression of creative needs and abilities. The stronger the needs and the higher the abilities, the more severe the pressures are likely to be. As a consequence, at each critical stage of development, many children sacrifice their creativity. For some, this may begin at age five. For others, it comes at age nine, or twelve, or at some later time. As they learn to cope with the new demands of a stage, some children recover while others apparently abandon their creativity, distort it, or hold tight reins on it. Evidence from many sources, however, suggests that we can assume a relatively optimistic outlook concerning the possibilities of reviving creativity at any age, with the proper conditions.

GIVING CHILDREN A CHANCE TO LEARN AND
THINK CREATIVELY

WHEN I ask parents and teachers if they want their children or pupils to learn and think creatively, I can count on most of them to say, "Yes!" But if I were to talk with them individually, or to observe their behavior toward children, I am afraid I would find that they don't *really* mean what they say. In mind and spirit they may approve of giving children a chance to learn and think creatively, but outwardly, in action, they behave in a contrary manner. So many parents and teachers feel uncomfortable, even disturbed, if their children display any tendencies to learn and think creatively. Such activity makes extra trouble for them. At times, the children are outright irritating; their eternal questions are often embarrassing. Many adults feel that children should assume their parents know everything that's worth knowing, instead of asking so many questions one can't answer.

There are many other reasons why parents discourage their children from learning, thinking, and behaving creatively. Perhaps the most important, however, is the fear that other people will think one's children are different or peculiar. Being different doesn't bother young children, but year by year they become more afraid of being individual, of being themselves. The awesomeness of being considered different or divergent is well understood by children in the fourth, fifth, and sixth grades. Its impact became clearest to me when we asked children to write imaginative stories about animals and people with characteristics that made them different.

Most revealing are the stories about the flying monkey. The parents of the flying monkey are upset when they learn that their son is a flying monkey. They may send him to another part of the jungle; they don't want him and reject him. They may think that he is mentally ill and take him to a doctor. Or, Mama may have Daddy give him a good talking to and tell him that the other animals will think he is crazy, if

NOTE: This chapter was originally a paper presented to the Southwood School PTA, Bloomington, Minnesota, November 28, 1961.

he continues to fly. They may tell the flying monkey that others will be afraid of him, or that he will have no friends. They may teach him how to hide or camouflage his wings, so that others will not know that he can fly. Or, they may cut his wings off. It is always the good little monkey who gives up his flying and other peculiar behavior. The following story of a flying monkey named Pepper is one of my favorites:

"Far in the jungle of Africa lived a flying monkey named Pepper. Pepper was a well-educated monkey and very cute . . . Pepper was unusual too. He was not like all of the other flying monkeys. You see, Pepper didn't eat bananas like everybody else. He wanted to be different. He ate peppers!

"No one ever went out of the jungle so Pepper, being different, decided to go to America! . . . When the people saw him, they began to laugh, and then others began to scream. Then out of nowhere a man from a zoo came and took Pepper by surprise. . . .

"Now Pepper was sad. He didn't like the cage they put him in. He made a vow that if he ever got out he would never be different again, and ten minutes later he saw some bent bars big enough to fly through. All of a sudden he flew out and in two days was back in the jungle. He kept his promise too. He was never different again. He was a good little flying monkey."

Pepper learned the hard way that it pays to conform and to eat one's bananas. Many parents, as did Pepper's, desperately want to prevent their children from suffering the painful experiences of being "different."

WHY BE CONCERNED?

Perhaps we can reinforce the desire of parents to give their children a chance to learn and think creatively by offering them the following reasons for doing so.

Mental Health. Parents want their children to enjoy good mental health. To help them avoid mental breakdowns, to help them develop their personalities in a healthy manner, are important concerns to any parent. I think there is little question but that the stifling of one's creative desires and abilities cuts at the very satisfaction in living and ultimately creates overwhelming tension and breakdown. There is also little doubt in my mind that the ability to learn and think creatively is our most valuable resource in coping with life's stresses and in maintaining our sanity.

Fully Functioning Persons. Parents want their children to become fully functioning persons, to develop all of their mental abilities. Much of our recent evidence suggests that the mental abilities involved in learning and thinking creatively are different from those used in learning by authority. When we learn by authority, we learn what we are told to learn and we accept it on authority because someone else tells us it is true. In learning by authority, the abilities measured by intelligence or **IQ** tests are important; primarily recognition, memory, and the reasoning abilities. To learn creatively we question, inquire, experiment, manipulate, or play with ideas and materials. This activity requires use of the mental abilities measured by tests of creative thinking, such as fluency, or the ability to think of a large number of ideas or possible solutions; flexibility, or the ability to think of different approaches or strategies; originality, or the ability to think of unusual possibilities, to get off the beaten track; and elaboration, or the ability to work out the details of an idea and implement it.

Certainly we cannot say that a child is fully functioning mentally, if the abilities involved in learning and thinking creatively remain undeveloped or are paralyzed by excessive prohibitions.

Educational Achievement. Parents and teachers want their children to learn in school. We have known for a long time that it is natural for man to want to learn creatively, but we have always considered it more economical to teach by authority. Recent experiments have shown that many things can be learned more economically by using creative ability than by relying on the passive reception of authority, and that some people can learn much creatively who learn little by authority.

Traditional tests of intelligence or scholastic aptitude have worked out rather well in predicting school achievement. The abilities measured by these tests are given almost exclusive emphasis when children are taught by authority. At the same time, however, other important kinds of achievement are not being measured or otherwise recognized in our schools. Recent and ongoing studies suggest that even the teaching of traditional subject matter and the traditional educational skills can be geared to encouraging intensive use of the creative thinking abilities.

Vocational Success. Parents want their children to succeed in their vocations. Creativity has long been recognized as a distinguishing characteristic of the outstanding contributors in almost every field. Possession of high intelligence, special talent, and technical skills is not alone sufficient. Scientific discovery, technological invention, and the humane arts ultimately depend upon creativity.

We are discovering now that creative thinking is essential to success even in relatively commonplace occupations, such as sales clerk in a department store (Wallace, 1961). One study found that saleswomen ranking in the upper third in sales in their departments scored higher on tests of creative thinking than those who ranked in the lower third. An interesting point, however, is that the tests do a better job of discriminating between the high and low selling groups in what the personnel manager considered routine sales jobs, requiring no imagination, than they do in departments rated as requiring creative thinking. Thus creative thinking may be a significant factor even in routine jobs.

Social Importance. Everyone wants his children to make useful contributions to society. We know that democracies collapse when they fail to use intelligent, imaginative methods for solving their problems. Greece failed to heed the warning of Socrates and gradually declined as a consequence. Children who are systematically conditioned for brainwashing can hardly be expected to work out solutions for our society's problems.

LEARNING AND THINKING CREATIVELY

What is meant by learning and thinking creatively? How does it differ from learning by authority? The answer seems simple and obvious, but its full meaning is extremely difficult to communicate. A child learns creatively by questioning, inquiring, searching, manipulating, experimenting, even by aimless play; in short, by always trying to get at the truth. Learning and thinking creatively take place in the process of sensing difficulties, problems, gaps in information; in making guesses or formulating hypotheses about these deficiencies; in testing these guesses and possibly revising and retesting them; and finally in communicating the results. Vital human needs are involved at each of these four stages. If we sense that something is missing or wrong, tension is aroused, we are uncomfortable, and to relieve our tension we try to make guesses in order to fill gaps and make connections. We know that our guesses may be wrong, but we find out how nearly they are correct, if at all. Thus we are driven to test our hypotheses, to modify them, to correct our errors. We cannot tolerate too much uncertainty. Once we make a discovery, we want to tell somebody about it. This is one reason why it is so natural for man to learn creatively.

We learn by authority when we are told what we should learn, when we accept an idea as true on the word of some authority, perhaps a teacher, a parent, a textbook, a newspaper, an encyclopedia, or the like. Authority frequently represents the majority opinion, the consensus of the peer group. We emphasize the importance of voting and the power of the majority so much that children may even seek to determine the truth by voting. Less conforming and more creative children, however, rebel at the voting approach to determine the truth. One mother of a highly creative child recently wrote me as follows:

"My second boy has a rigid, peer-oriented person for a teacher and she is never encouraging to her class to deviate from the accepted, standard way of doing things . . . What the GROUP thinks is important to her, and they vote on everything. My son says he hates to vote and hopes he never has to again. What an attitude to develop in second graders!"

To help me communicate this concept, I should like to present a series of verbal pictures that show children learning and thinking creatively, and how parents and teachers so easily and frequently disrupt and destroy the creative thinking and learning process. We know this process tends to be quick, automatic, and spontaneous. The trouble is that we do so many things to interrupt it.

The First Day with Rhythm Band Instruments. Imagine a class of first graders on the first day they are given their rhythm band instruments. On this occasion, most teachers are driven to distraction. Wanting to talk about the instruments and how they work, they usually fail to hold the attention of the children. Not so, the teacher of this first grade class. She has learned that the children must first be permitted to encounter their instruments creatively. They want to feel them, smell them, look at them, tap them, and sense them in every way possible. They must find out at once what the instruments will do. After this, they are *ready* to learn by authority.

Here the creative learning and thinking process would have been cut off if the teacher had tried to hurry and push the children, to force them to get on with what she wanted to teach them — how to use the instruments properly. We curb their creative impulses when we try to prepare children like these excited band pupils through a verbal or authoritarian orientation, or when we try to sustain an unnatural dichotomy between work and play. Some principals and parents would be gravely disturbed by the behavior of these children. They would say this must be a play school, that the children are learning nothing — just playing, clowning, acting up.

Parents and teachers also throw off course the thinking processes through the condescending way they talk with children, asking questions but not giving them an opening for an answer. One mother describes how shocked she was when her five-year-old daughter expressed her desire to eat alone in her room because the mother was having a friend over for lunch (Miller, 1961). The child said she didn't like to talk with Mrs. Green.

When pressed to explain, she said, "Oh, you know. She talks to me in a baby voice — and keeps asking me things and never lets me answer."

Then the mother recalled that every remark Mrs. Green made to the child was some little question she obviously did not expect answered. "Where did you get that pretty dress? What have you been doing today? What makes Julie grow so fast?"

The child not responding, Mrs. Green would make matters worse by adding: "My, Julie is a shy one, isn't she? Are you bashful, honey? She doesn't talk much, does she?"

Many highly creative children appear to be either shy or show-offs. Shy children will talk freely with adults, if they are given time to answer questions — time to think and to find words to express their ideas. The show-offs will find their acting up unnecessary if they are accepted as persons in conversations with adults.

Sitting and Thinking. Imagine a kindergarten boy sitting alone, apparently lost in thought. This is a disturbing sight, for the ideal pupil, even a kindergartener, is industrious; he must keep busy at all times. At first the boy's apparent detachment concerned me greatly. I had administered a task in which I had shown how one could take a triangular piece of colored paper and make it the roof of a bird house. I then said, "Now don't you make a bird house. This was just an example. Think of something different." This boy delayed beginning much longer than the other children. He had been sitting and thinking how a bird house would look on the inside, and that is what he drew.

If I had gone over to urge him to get busy, I would have interrupted his thinking and he would doubtless have produced either nothing or something very obvious and banal. It is necessary to give children time to think, and to make thinking a legitimate activity. We are so accustomed to believing that the good child is a busy child, an industrious child, that we suspect he is up to some mischief if he is not visibly engaged in some approved activity. Robert Frost was dropped from school for what we call daydreaming; during some of his lapses from attention he was probably revolving a poem in his mind. Other eminent creative writers, scientists, and inventors have had similar experiences.

Parents and teachers would do well to check themselves occasionally, for a day or two, on how many times they throw off course a child's thinking — or how many times they are tempted to do so, if they can resist. A father who ran this check stopped himself as he was about to show his son the "right" way to stack his blocks — large ones on the bottom, small ones on top (Weisbord, 1961). He also caught himself as he was about to tell the child to stop playing with the Venetian blind cord and to correct his method for holding — of all things — a ukelele. I am sure that good parents have similar impulses all day long. With a moment's thought this father recognized that there is no "right" way to stack blocks and that an eighteen-month-old cannot hold a ukelele the way an adult does. He also recognized that the Venetian blind cord meant something different to his son than to an adult and that the boy wasn't hurting himself, or the blind, or interfering with the father by pulling the blind cord. Why then was the father on the verge of making him stop? Certainly one has to hold certain limits, but most parents will be surprised at how many things they unnecessarily forbid, thereby interfering with healthy kinds of learning and thinking.

A Closer Look. An attractive kindergarten boy is using a magnifying glass to get a closer look at some sea shells. Much creative learning and thinking takes place in the science corners of the primary grades. Here children can freely examine many of the wonders of the world, ask questions, and — most important — find out things for themselves.

The child needs to see for himself. There is simply no satisfactory substitute for personal observation. If we watch a child, we will note that he is content to observe an object at a distance only for a while. Looking from a distance, however, does not satisfy his curiosity. He wants to see things up close. Creative learning and thinking lose scope when children are denied that important closer look, when they must not touch, when they are given no real chance to encounter so many exciting things in their environment.

Teachers and parents place many restrictions on the child's natural desire to manipulate things, on his curiosity. This almost irresistible tendency of the child to manipulate and explore objects seems to be the basis of curiosity and inventiveness in the adult. Even in individual testing situations we find that the children who do the most manipulating of objects think of the most ideas and of the most original ideas.

More manipulative than girls, boys become increasingly so from the first through the third grade. To develop creative thinking, even to permit children to learn effectively, I believe they must be encouraged to manipulate, to play imaginatively with objects and ideas, as much as possible within the limits of safety.

Parents may be inconvenienced occasionally, and may not appreciate a child's passion for firsthand observation. Broken objects about the house — soap broken into bits, an egg beater taken apart, the bristles torn out of a brush — may be misinterpreted as signs of childish meanness. The child's eagerness to understand a bird's nesting habits and to see the mother feeding her young may lead to damaged shrubbery and broken tree branches. It might help if we could redefine behavior of this kind. In one school, we administered a battery of creative thinking tasks and a questionnaire in which we asked: Who in your class thinks of a lot of good ideas? Who does the most talking? Who thinks of a lot of ideas for being naughty? Later one of the teachers told me that my research had helped the teachers a great deal, whether I had found out anything or not. Our tests had changed their way of perceiving behavior: "We no longer look upon children as naughty but as thinking of ideas for being naughty." Parents will be surprised at the difference this attitude will make in their reaction to children's behavior.

Resources and Limitations. Let us now imagine a series of pictures in this same kindergarten. Three children are sailing a boat constructed from large blocks and a white rag on a stick. Two girls are talking over toy telephones. Several children are standing at easels, painting pictures with bright colors. These materials are intended to stimulate imaginative role-playing, an important way for children to test their abilities and learn verbal, social, and other skills. Deprived of the materials needed to carry out their ideas, children become frustrated.

We realize, however, that we can never provide children with all the resources they need in carrying out their ideas. Instead, we must teach them a creative rather than cynical acceptance of limitations. In the next picture, a first grade girl has made an exciting model of a man in a boat, on a lake, catching a big fish. The model was made from items selected from a burlap bag full of junk, which her teacher keeps in the cloakroom. The bag contains odds and ends — sticks, scraps of cloth, the rollers from toilet paper, and the like. About once a week, she turns her first graders loose on these materials to see what they can make.

Some people may be bothered by our kindergarten scenes and may derisively view them as typical of a play school. There we see children engaging in fantasy, a practice regarded by many parents and teachers as unhealthy, to be eliminated. We may try too early, however, to eliminate fantasy from the thinking of children. Imaginative role-playing, telling fantastic stories, and making unusual drawings should be considered as normal aspects of a child's thinking. Certainly we are interested in a sound type of creativity, but it seems to me that we must keep fantasy alive until the child's intellectual development is such that he can engage in sound creative thinking. In our testing of first and second graders we have seen indications that many children with impoverished imaginations have been subjected to some rather vigorous and stern efforts to eliminate fantasy too early.

Certainly, parents and teachers need to teach children early how to test their ideas against reality. The lack of verification or revision of ideas is the major difference between the imaginative thinking of the mental patient and the creative thought of the healthy person. Such training is also a safeguard against much so-called creativity which can be legitimately regarded with suspicion. Ability to test ideas will protect us from brainwashing, hidden persuaders, Communism, and other threatening influences.

What I would like to emphasize by means of these kindergarten situations is the importance of making available to children the necessary resources for carrying out creative ideas. Otherwise, frustration and a feeling of purposelessness are likely to result. There is value in the excitement of seeing the embodiment of one's idea, in some concrete form or product, even if only in a model of the idea or invention. It is obvious, however, that homes, schools, and even communities are unable to provide all the resources children need to realize and bring to life their ideas. I find that the lack of resources for working out ideas hampers the imagination at all educational levels. The graduate students I teach are greatly inhibited in developing new ideas and in planning research. Many of our third graders comment that they could think of more ideas for improving the toys used in our experiments but that the improvements would make them cost too much.

Parents can do a great deal to help their children accept creatively the unavailability of resources and learn to improvise. There is an important difference between accepting limitations cynically and accepting them creatively. This principle is illustrated by three examples of responses to the problem of improving the toy fire truck. Many describe elaborate and expensive hose arrangements that squirt water. Some say, "I could think of something but it would cost too much," and refuse to present ideas. Others describe arrangements for using a piece of string or a stick as a hose. In the first example, the child's imagination is unhampered by a lack of resources. In the second, the child accepts limitations cynically, is frozen, and produces no ideas. In the third, the child accepts limitations creatively and uses the resources available to serve his purpose of "having more fun."

Creativity Begets Creativity. Imagine a class of thirty-five fifth and sixth graders with a menagerie of the oddest assortment of papier-mâché animals ever seen. One of the girls is holding her prize animal, named Petrified Rosebud. She has written an enchanting, entertaining, and original story explaining how this animal acquired its unusual name. The really interesting thing about this whole activity is that all thirty-five stories written by these children were exciting, entertaining, and original. In creating these animals over a period of several days they had become so caught up in the process of creative thinking that it was easy to write such stories. Anyone familiar with the usual compositions of fifth and sixth graders will realize how remarkable this occurrence is. It is a case of creativity begetting creativity. We have too few sustained creative activities in which one project is permitted to lead to another. Usually, each classroom activity must be completed within a fixed twenty- or thirty-minute period.

Not even parents can deliver children from the tyranny of the clock, but in many ways they have more latitude than teachers in which to provide sustained activities with the possibility of one thing leading naturally to another. There are times when we cannot hurry the process of learning and thinking creatively. We may strain and work hard to think of a new idea, we may want to think of one in the worst way, and still be unable to produce anything. Then suddenly it comes — while we are shaving, taking a bath, or sitting in church. The principle involved here can even be applied to the problem of answering questions. Although we cannot expect children to delay very long in responding to questions, parents and teachers can do much to enrich the period between the question and the answer. Children need to learn how to sustain a question, to play with it, toss it back and forth, refine it, and accept the questioning mood without ready-made answers from adults.

Learning from the Creativity of Nature. Now, imagine a class of thirty kindergarteners making butter. The teacher has poured some cream in a fruit jar and let the children pass it from one to another, each giving it a shake. After a few rounds they have butter, which they sample with delight. Children are curious about natural processes and need to experience them.

I am quite excited about the contribution of the science and art camps, a movement which seems to be gaining momentum under the auspices of the Science Arts Camps, Inc. At one camp I visited I asked the children what was different about the way they learned at camp and the way they learned at school. The element that came out over and over again in our interviews was the difference in their relationship to their instructors. These children had greater respect for their teachers at camp than for their teachers at school. They said the camp teachers were not bossy, more friendly, smarter, nicer, more interesting, more understanding and not goody-goody, more free, and the like. At school, there was no time for "fascinating experiments." It is true that the camp teachers were of high caliber, each strongly committed to his field of art or science.

We know of course that the active mind of the child exposed to nature will ask questions, draw invalid conclusions, and often associate scraps of information that have no connection. For example, one six-year-old after a visit to a farm told his little friend, "We went to the farm Sunday. I saw the baby cows and big cows. The baby cows don't like their mothers, so they are tied up in the barn and can't run around and play. I don't think the little cows are happy" (Weinlander, 1959). Even young children, however, can be taught to sift facts from fiction and to test their guesses about the laws of nature. Such testing of ideas can dispel many superstitions and fears. I believe the greatest interference with the child's learning and thinking creatively comes from his being removed from the ever creative processes of nature.

Writing Down Ideas. A class of third graders are busy writing stories. Some are sitting in corners by themselves, others in clusters of four or two or three. No one has his feet flat on the floor. Some are even sitting on their feet. Others have their knees where their seats should be or in other contorted positions. Such disorder would drive some principals frantic even though the children are quiet, deeply absorbed in their storywriting. I feel sure they would be far less creative if made to sit in straight rows with their feet flat on the floor.

Children are natural storytellers and can write charmingly and excitingly, if encouraged to do so. I am always amazed at the richness of the stories children write at a moment's notice even when given only twenty minutes to think up and write them. Parents can do much to help their children learn how to express their thoughts and observations in writing. Children do not usually begin to write about events on their own initiative (Weinlander, 1959). They need guidance and suggestions on how to organize and keep records of their experiences.

Parents, as well as teachers, should be warned against placing too much emphasis on mechanics while children are learning to record their experiences. Creativeness may be dampened by overattention to neatness, spelling, and writing, or by insistence on copying models. The originality of children is impaired when they write something to be corrected rather than something to be simply read and enjoyed.

A great deal of pleasure lies in store for parents in the original writings of their children. Given sufficient attention and shown genuine appreciation, children feel free to be creative and spontaneous in their writing.

INTERFERENCE WITH CREATIVITY

Many social pressures stressed at home and in the community interfere with the creative processes. Consider our excessive emphasis on a success-orientation—our exaggerated fear of making mistakes. Over-emphasis or misplaced emphasis on sex roles also exacts a heavy toll on the creative thinking of both boys and girls. Consider too our tendency to overrate the finished product, the great work of art, the harmonious interpersonal relationship, the well-organized behavior of a group. We fail to note the struggles through which these achievements came into being. We stress the importance of verbal skills, especially writing. We give credit frequently only for what an individual can write down, not recognizing that not all thinking expresses itself in verbal form. We place great emphasis upon what one knows rather than upon his attitude toward what he knows or what he can do with what he knows.

We cannot place all the blame on teachers and schools. Schools reflect the values of the home and the community; they are not likely to stimulate creative thinking or tolerate divergency any more than the community. For this reason, we are interested in studying the attitudes of different cultures toward divergency. We have asked thousands of children to write imaginative stories about animals or persons with some divergent characteristic. We believe that these materials reveal the child's perceptions of the ways his society deals with divergency. As social psychologists have discovered through experimental work, divergency is subjected to tremendous pressure in almost all cultures. Pressures come from different sources, are handled differently from culture to culture, and are stronger in some cultures or subcultures than in others. For example, pressures are stronger in urban areas than in rural areas, in regular mixed classes than in special classes for the gifted, in parochial schools than in public schools. In most of the American children's stories, the source of pressure tends to be one's peers. In the Canadian stories, however, it is society in general. Pressure in the American stories takes the form of ridicule or laughter, coercion, and isolation; in the Greek stories, questioning, verbal advice, and suggestions that medical treatment might help; in the stories of American Negro children in nonsegregated schools, hostility and violence, ridicule, and coercion. The Greek stories show great concern about understanding the causes of divergency; the Canadian stories, about understanding the external social causation. Little such concern is found in the American stories; divergency is divergency and cause matters not.

To achieve the happiness and security they naturally want for their children, parents tend to reinforce the pressures of the culture toward conformity. Many parents go to extreme lengths, like the mother who started doing her child's homework for him. When asked why, she replied, "I don't want him to get hurt by failing." In this way, parents rob their children of curiosity, initiative, and resourcefulness. All children learn by trial and error, by guessing and testing, by failing and trying again. There are special joys in solving a problem entirely by oneself. We should remind ourselves that the child strives for independence from the time he learns to crawl.

REWARDING CREATIVE THINKING

Repeatedly I have said that we must reward creative thinking, if we expect to challenge gifted children to learn and think creatively. The problem of rewarding creative talent is indeed a difficult one, for which our society has not yet worked out a good solution. Although much of our research at the University of Minnesota has been devoted to this problem, and although we have conducted experiments to test a number of specific ideas, I shall limit myself here to setting forth five principles for rewarding creative thinking.

Treat Unusual Questions with Respect. Nothing is more rewarding to the questioning child than an adequate answer. Questions reflect a "mind hunger" that must be satisfied lest the mind starve. Although the need should be met immediately, the period between the question and the answer can often be given to fruitful thought and discussion. In general, we should tell children only what they cannot learn for themselves. This means that the parent or teacher who sets out to be respectful and considerate must be prepared for some shocks. That children will ask many unanswerable questions should be accepted as normal and desirable. Adults who respond with threats and evasions lose the enjoyment of a mutual searching for solutions to the questions children raise. Parents and teachers should not be afraid to let children guess freely, right or wrong, about answers and solutions, but should encourage them to analyze and seek to verify their guesses, on the basis of their own observations and experience.

Treat Unusual Ideas with Respect. Children who are stimulated by the creative approach see many relationships and significances that their parents and teachers miss. They express ideas that parents and teachers are unable to evaluate. Because it is extremely difficult to reward such thinking properly, our more creatively talented youngsters are the least rewarded for their effort.

A workshop group in Toronto recently criticized this principle, suggesting it should be changed to read: "Stimulate unusual or original ideas." I reiterate, however, that we should not stimulate such thinking unless we are prepared to be respectful of it. Certainly we shall not continue to elicit original thinking if we seem unable to respect it.

Show Children that Their Ideas Have Value. To the many adults who feel that children are incapable of producing ideas of any value I would suggest only that they try to alert themselves to recognize unusual and worthwhile ideas among children. Children can be shown that their ideas have value, if we discuss them with understanding, if we display them, if we give credit for them. There is also the matter of intrinsic rewards. Much is said about the role of reward and punishment in learning, but little about the lure of discovery and the role of curiosity and interest, an area where rewards have been neglected.

Provide Opportunities for Self-Initiated Learning and Give Credit for It. An old principle of learning is: "Excite and direct the self-activities of the learner, and tell him nothing that he can learn for himself." One mark of the highly creative person is his self-starting ability. The strong curiosity and exploratory tendencies of the child suggest that all or almost all children are self-starting. The problem of parents and teachers is to keep this ability alive, because it is hindered by overdetailed supervision. Perhaps too much reliance is placed upon prescribed curricula; perhaps we need more effort to appraise and credit growth resulting from the student's own initiative. We might do better to teach fewer subjects and allow more time for self-initiated learning, for thinking creatively about the subjects taught.

The reason for evaluating and crediting self-initiated learning and thinking seems quite simple. Because grades are important to students, they tend to learn whatever is necessary to obtain desirable grades. If we base our evaluation on the memorization of details, students will memorize the texts and lectures. If we base grades upon ability to integrate and apply principles, students will attempt to perform accordingly. If we give credit for the development of original ideas and for self-initiated activities, achievement along these lines will be forthcoming.

Provide Periods of Nonevaluated Practice or Learning. We do not have to evaluate everything. Children need periods in which they can learn without the threat of being evaluated. External evaluation is always a threat and creates a need for defensiveness, and prevents some portion of the child's experiencing or sensing from achieving full awareness. What is lost is the openness that is so necessary to the production of new ideas. In our experiments we find consistent validation for this principle of nonevaluation in the first, second, and third grades. A one-hour laboratory task, however, did not yield the expected results in the fourth, fifth, and sixth grades. It may be that by the time a child reaches the fourth grade he is so conditioned to being evaluated and is so dependent upon external evaluation that he is not released by being told that the initial learning and exploratory phase is not graded or scored. I believe that we must first demonstrate to these older children that practice really is off the record, before they will respond to the nonevaluative condition.

CONCLUSION

I should like to urge all parents to cooperate with the school as it seeks to help the child realize his creativeness, as it introduces new tests for special abilities and aptitudes. It may be two or three years before tests of the creative thinking abilities will be as common as tests of intelligence or IQ now are. The time will soon come, however. I hope that parents will not be disturbed by assignments that require the child to use his imagination in applying facts, not to memorize or merely organize facts. I hope that parents will support the school when it starts giving examinations that require creative thinking in addition to those that emphasize recall and recognition of facts.

Parents need not be disturbed if a child shows little inclination to become a walking scientific encyclopedia. I would urge them instead to be concerned about what kind of child he is becoming. What kind of thinking does he do? How resourceful is he? Can he direct his own goals and initiate his own learning? Is he learning to give thoughtful explanations of things he sees, hears, and does? Does he consider his ideas important? Does he relate similar experiences together to draw conclusions? Does he do some thinking for himself? Parents can ask themselves these questions as a guide to helping the child develop his creative thinking potentialities.

CREATIVE STUDENTS IN OUR SCHOOLS TODAY

THE stories of the following eight creative students show what current research is discovering about the identification of creative students, what makes them different from their classmates, and what happens to them in school. I have chosen these eight by no means unique cases to represent the most frequently occurring types of creative student from kindergarten through college. The names are fictitious, but their histories are authentic. The research findings discussed in relation to these students are based on fairly large numbers, usually the total population of at least two schools.

OLLIE, A KINDERGARTEN BOY

Ollie is a kindergarten boy in a suburban school. I have shown Ollie's picture, taken as he sat thinking during one of our experiments, to hundreds of teachers and parents. Almost all have guessed that Ollie is daydreaming; only rarely does anyone say, "Maybe he's thinking." The sight Ollie presents is disturbing to many of us because we place so much value on a child's being visibly industrious; other behavior we tend to label daydreaming, loafing, or mischief-making. When I first encountered him, in a class of thirty-three children to which I was administering a battery of nonverbal tasks in creative thinking, Ollie irritated me like the very devil. In giving the Picture Construction Task, I had shown the class how a colored triangle could be used as the roof of a bird house. I had drawn the house, a hole for the birds to fly in and out, and some other objects to make it tell a story. I told them, "Now, don't draw what I did. Try to think of something no one else in the class will think of. Then add other things to make it tell a story." Thirty-one of these children were eager to start; they could hardly wait for me to finish the instructions. After about a minute, one of the two delayers started to work on his idea. Ollie, however, just sat there, gazing before him. Afraid he might not have understood the instructions, that he might be uncooper-

NOTE: This chapter was originally a paper presented at the Metropolitan School Study Council, Horace Mann Auditorium, Teachers College, Columbia University, New York, April 10, 1962.

ative or angry, I made a start at least a dozen times to approach him, to urge him to get busy, but I waited. Finally, he began to work with great vigor and enthusiasm. I discovered later that Ollie had been thinking about how a bird house would look on the inside, which he attempted to picture in his drawing. Since then, I have not encountered a single other person who has ever thought about the interior appearance of a bird house, much less draw it.

There are other reasons why I think Ollie is a creative child. He showed much originality, flexibility, elaboration, and a fair degree of fluency on other tests of creative thinking, including the following three nonverbal tasks:

1. The Picture Construction Task. Different shapes of gummed paper are used as the stimulus material: a triangle, a kidney shape, and a teardrop shape. Productions are scored for originality and elaboration and the instructions are designed to evoke these two qualities.

2. The Incomplete Figures Task. An incomplete figure sets up tensions in the viewer and there is a tendency to complete the figure in the most direct way possible — by a straight line, curve, or circle. Resisting this tendency, delaying gratification, permits one to make greater mental leaps and results in more original, more flexible, and more elaborate products. Ollie, even as a kindergartener, made such leaps. Incidentally, highly creative children *can* sit still longer, *can* wait longer, than less creative children. Under the guise of administering children an aptitude test for space travel, Singer found that the more imaginative subjects could sit still and wait longer than their less imaginative age mates (Singer, 1961).

3. The Circle Task. Confronted with thirty-five circles, Ollie was asked to sketch objects or pictures that have a circle as a major part. The instructions stress the need for fluency (sketch as many objects as possible), flexibility (different kinds of objects), originality (objects no one else in the class will think of), and elaboration (add details to make it tell a story). Ollie's performance was especially noted for originality and flexibility, even though fluency and elaboration were also high.

In an individual testing situation, Ollie was administered two verbal tasks: the Ask-and-Guess Test and the Product Improvement and Unusual Uses Test. In the Ask-and-Guess Test, he was shown a picture illustrating the Ding Dong Bell nursery rhyme and instructed to ask as many questions as he could about the action shown, answers to which could not be found in the picture. He was then asked to make guesses about previous events that might have led up to the pictured event, and finally to make guesses about possible events that might follow as a consequence. In the Product Improvement and Unusual Uses Test he was handed a stuffed toy dog and asked to suggest ways of improving the toy to make it more fun to play with. After this, he was asked to think of other uses of the toy dog, other than as something to play with, either as it was or as it might be changed.

While taking the Product Improvement Test, Ollie examined the toy thoroughly. He smelled it, rubbed it, held it in different positions, shook it, almost taking it apart. With each new examination, a new idea seemed to flow from his mind. This is characteristic of highly creative children. The least creative children immediately put the toy back on the examiner's table, as though afraid they would be hurt by it, and give few responses, usually of an obvious and commonplace type. Most children will hold the toy, look at it in various positions, and give a larger number of responses — and more original responses — than those who put the toy down, but fewer and less original responses than children like Ollie.

Is the kind of performance represented by Ollie useful in identifying creative students? Will Ollie be a creative adult? Can one object that I am using a loose definition of creativity or creative thinking and that such terms should be used only to refer to what goes on in the minds of indisputably creative people? I am familiar with and have considered many such arguments and suggestions, and would answer them in the following way.

First, whether Ollie becomes a creative adult will depend in a large measure upon how we, representing school and society, treat his curiosity needs and how much we interfere with those quick, automatic processes that now characterize him. Art teachers have observed that the drawing and painting techniques of young children are more like those of professional artists than are those of older children or adolescents. Vocal behavior of infants and young children is likewise similar to that of great vocal artists, more so than that of adults.

Second, when the same tests are given to graduate students, the kind of performance displayed by Ollie, similar in approach, behavior, and techniques, differentiates the students with highly original ideas from their less creative peers, whose ideas are judged as obvious, commonplace, and banal. This kind of performance also differentiates highly creative students in industrial design courses from their less creative peers, saleswomen who sell most from those who sell least, high school students who are nominated by their classmates on some criterion of creativity from those who are not, children who are nominated by their teachers on one of these criteria from those who are not, children who score low on tests of attitudinal rigidity from those who score high, and children who initiate a large number of ideas in group problem-solving tasks from those who initiate few.

The test-retest reliability at the kindergarten level, and for the first, second, and third grades, is not as high as I should like. The reliabilities for retesting at one year intervals drop to the .30's for some of the individual tasks and are in the .50's and .60's for battery totals. Above the fourth grade, test-retest reliabilities for total batteries range from the high .50's to the high .80's. I am not especially worried about this, since my own chief interest is in evoking and developing whatever creative talents a child possesses. I know full well that creative performance depends heavily upon home and school conditions, the response to creative needs, and whether creative thinking and creative achievement are rewarded or discouraged. Knowing what happens to most children like Ollie, we can hardly expect high test-retest reliability on any test of creative thinking.

Actually, Ollie fares rather well in his school. His teacher permits him and his classmates to engage in fantasy activities. She believes in keeping fantasy alive until their mental development allows them to engage in a sounder type of creative thinking. She indulges their curiosity, their inclination to take a closer look. She provides them with materials and projects with which to experiment and play freely. She guides them in thinking up and making products that bring the group reward and recognition. She keeps them in contact with the creative processes of nature by letting them make butter, grow plants, and observe the transformation of a cocoon into a moth.

ANNE, ANOTHER KINDERGARTENER

Anne and many other highly creative kindergarteners are not so fortunate as Ollie. Anne also attracted my attention in the testing situation. Her responses were quicker than Ollie's and her ideational fluency more superior. Near the end of the ten-minute Circles Task, I announced, "You have one more minute before your time is up." Anne still had two lines of circles she had not used. She immediately drew a girl blowing bubbles, making the uncompleted circles represent the bubbles.

Anne's kindergarten teacher is quite different from Ollie's. To her, creative behavior in children is irritating, not to be tolerated. Doing one's work on time, accepting the teacher's word, consideration of others, obedience, and industry are greatly rewarded. Interrupting or disturbing the class procedure, attempting difficult tasks, always asking questions, wanting to work alone, spirited disagreement, and fault-finding are sternly discouraged.

According to Anne's father, she was extremely excited about learning at the time she entered kindergarten:

"She had been anxious all summer, even though I kept reminding her that she would not be allowed to read until a year later, in the first grade . . . The first few weeks of kindergarten she was delirious with excitement. Every day she was eager for school. Show and Tell time was her favorite. She collected leaves from twenty-two different varieties of trees in the yard. Then she pasted them in a book, printed their names underneath and took them for Show and Tell with an explanation of what makes leaves change color. Next, she took her pet turtle with her book illustrating the life cycles of fishes, reptiles and amphibians.

"About November she began to complain that all of the other kids were bringing their toys and dolls for Show and Tell or telling what they saw on TV. Her interest dropped further as she found that the teacher did all of the reading instead of letting the kids read. The end came when the teacher refused to let her use the Teach-a-Time clock to show the other kids how to tell time and made her paste paper instead. Her interests then began to move in the direction of what she wore that was different from other children. She began to quote more and more what the teacher said and accepted it over anything else.

"Interest was revived briefly when the teacher said she could bring her telescope and book on astronomy during the week they were to talk about outer space. However, the teacher did not understand her explanation of how a reflecting type telescope works and pointed the wrong end at the sun during an observation attempt. By this time, she accepted the teacher's word to the point where she was afraid to correct the teacher and turn the telescope around. From that day on she has refused to bring another thing for Show and Tell and began talking only of when the next school vacation would begin."

Perhaps in cases such as Anne's we have the beginning of the drop-out problem, about which we are beginning to hear a great deal.

Apparently, Anne's story is not an unusual one. Many of the letters I have received from mothers of kindergarten children relate similar accounts. Research shows that as a group five-year-olds register a drop in their measured creative thinking ability and in observed imaginative behavior (Andrews, 1930). Fortunately, most of them recover, show gains between five and six, and continue to show gains until about age nine, at least in the United States. It is about those who do not recover that we should be concerned.

KEITH, A SEVENTH GRADER

Although I recognize the fallibility of accounts by parents, I should like to sketch briefly Keith's story as told by his mother. Before Keith entered school, everyone was impressed by his curiosity, cleverness, and mature thinking. Strangers would assume that he was in the third or fourth grade at the time he was four and a half years old. When Keith brought home his corrected kindergarten papers, his mother was disturbed to find that he was doing failing work. He would add cowboy hats or boots to the dittoed drawings his teacher gave him to color or even more radically change a drawing. The trend seems to have continued throughout the remainder of Keith's educational career. His parents have had Keith tested by some of the best pediatricians in their area. All have said that there is nothing wrong with Keith either physically or mentally and that he will learn when he has the "right teacher." Now thirteen years old, Keith was retained in the seventh grade last year, and teachers suspect that he is mentally retarded. His parents wonder. They see him come alive and work enthusiastically with projects at home and cannot believe that he is mentally retarded. Instead of talking about when the next school vacation will begin, as Anne does, Keith talks about when he will be old enough to drop out of school.

JIM, A THIRD GRADER

Jim, perhaps one of the most inventive and creative children we have tested during the past four years, was one of his school's most serious problems, in spite of his outstanding intellectual talents (IQ 135). The teacher, the principal, the school social worker, the school psychologist, and the parents were all concerned. One aspect of Jim's case is reported in a preceding chapter, where his failure to learn to read, his classmates' low opinion of his abilities, and his performance indicating withdrawal on the House-Tree-Person Test are described (see pp. 34–35).

In the fourth grade, Jim changed schools and had in his class several other highly creative children. Here he was less deviate than he had been in his third grade class and his classmates respected him for his ideas. Although Jim's fourth grade teacher did not encourage many creative activities, and the creative thinking abilities — as measured by our tests — dropped for Jim and his classmates, he did not have to sacrifice his creativity but found outlets for it in experiments at home and with some of the boys in his class. Furthermore, he learned to read. His fifth grade teacher encouraged creative thinking somewhat more than his fourth grade teacher, especially in the area of science where Jim showed strong enthusiasm. Although observers noted that his classmates were usually pleased when Jim made a mistake or expressed an idea judged to be "too wild" by the teacher, there was no question of their high respect for him. His physical growth was very rapid during the fourth and fifth grade and he was perhaps the best athlete in the class. During the latter part of the fifth grade he was elected president of the class. In all areas his achievement was well above the norms for his class at the end of the fifth grade. His achievement in reading skills was about the middle of the eighth grade; language skills, about the middle of the ninth; arithmetic concepts and problem-solving, near the top of the tenth grade; and arithmetic computation, middle of the seventh.

The intelligent concern of parents, teachers, and other school officials has guided Jim past some of the danger points in his creative development. Although problems of adjustment remain, although it will be a struggle for him to maintain his creativity, Jim is at least now achieving the educational skills necessary to the future pursuit of his interests in scientific discovery and invention. He has also overcome much of his estrangement from his peers and teachers. These advances will perhaps save him from delinquency and psychosis, both of which seemed likely when I first met Jim.

BOB, A FOURTH GRADER

I first met Bob when he was in the fourth grade. On the group-administered test of creative thinking he achieved one of the lowest scores in his class. He was at the top of his class, however, on the individually administered battery. The examiner noted, "This boy is terrific! He reminds me of the kind of person who as a big executive can dictate to five secretaries at the same time without becoming confused. After each task was given, he sat and dictated responses without interruption until time was called." Analysis of the responses for flexibility, originality, and elaboration revealed that his was a superior performance.

Upon investigation, it was found that Bob had been one of his school's most serious problems for the past two years. He was having difficulty learning to read and usually turned in papers that were almost blanks. His teacher's curiosity, however, was aroused by the discrepancy between his written and oral response. The teacher began asking Bob more questions and listening to his ideas. To the teacher's amazement, Bob was learning more than the teacher had imagined and was capable of a higher level of thinking than he had dreamed. Similar cases were found in several fourth grade classes studied during the early phases of our research. When teachers started looking at these children differently, giving them understanding and encouragement, their behavior changed accordingly.

I next noticed Bob in our experiments on homogeneous and heterogeneous grouping for creative activities. At the time Bob was in the fourth grade we divided his classroom group heterogeneously into five five-person groups on the basis of total scores on a battery of creative thinking tasks. Bob worked alone on the Science Toy Task, which required the groups first to experiment and explore in order to discover as many as possible intended and unintended uses of the science toys and then to demonstrate the toys and explain the scientific principles upon which they work. The other four members of his group worked in pairs but consulted Bob several times during the exploratory session. Bob said very little during the explanations until everyone else bogged down; he would then show the others what to do or explain the scientific principle involved.

When Bob was in the fifth grade we divided his class homogeneously according to the results of a group test of creative thinking. This placed Bob in the lowest ability group. A prize was offered to the group producing the largest number of ideas and explaining the largest number of principles. The task was similar to that used the previous year but the toys were entirely different. Bob's group entered into the activity with great enthusiasm. It was clear to the observer that their preferred method of learning was through experimentation, exploration, and trial-and-error. Occasionally they arrived at principles but were unable to articulate them. Even so, the performance of this low-ability group was clearly superior to that of the other four groups, which were of higher ability.

The performance of Bob and his group was not unusual. Using the results from two schools in which classes were grouped homogeneously and heterogeneously, all-out performance on the part of the lowest ability groups was the rule rather than the exception. In heterogeneous groups, individuals of differing measured ability behaved according to expectations. The trend was definitely linear on number of ideas initiated, but no such linear trend held for measured ability when homogeneous grouping was used. The lowest ability groups tended to outdo the highest ability groups. Similar results were obtained on number of ideas demonstrated and explained. Here, however, low-ability group members tended to come through for their groups when everyone else bogged down, just as Bob did for his group. Morever, social stress was reduced when the groups were divided homogeneously. Apparently the decrease in divergency in homogeneous groupings results in less fighting and other disruptive behavior and more encouraging, cooperative, and positive interaction.

Reducing the social stress that results from divergency seems to be quite important in the fourth, fifth, and sixth grades. In one experiment we studied the effects of various kinds of peer evaluation and discussion following a practice task in creative thinking, in the interval before moving on to a test task. After one practice task, the class was asked to discuss one another's work critically; after a second, to discuss only other possibilities that might have made the ideas developed more interesting, unusual, original, and communicative. The two treatments produced no differences in kindergarten through the third grade. Creative performance on the test task following the critical discussion by peers, however, was significantly inhibited in the fourth, fifth, and sixth grades. When the evaluative discussion was conducted by the adult experimenter, essentially opposite results were obtained. Unevaluated practice compared with evaluated practice improved creative performance in the lower grades but made no difference in the fourth, fifth, and sixth grades.

A plausible explanation of these results is found in development psychology, in what we know about the age at which peer approval and consensual validation become increasingly important. Further explanation is offered by a recent experiment of ours on peer and adult influences on problem-solving. Early in the morning we gave the well-known Maier's Horse-Trading Problem (Maier and Solem, 1952) to the third, fourth, and fifth grades in one school. That afternoon we readministered the problem and asked the children to check whether or not they had discussed the problem meanwhile with another member of their class, the teacher or some other adult in the school, or someone in a higher grade. In the third grade only 21 per cent reported discussing the problem with a classmate, but the percentage rose to 48 in the fourth and 67 in the fifth. Thirty-five per cent of the third grade, however, reported discussing the problem with some adult, while only 14 per cent of the fourth and 16 per cent of the fifth did so. Among other things, this probably helps to explain the drop in creative functioning in the fourth grade. In Western Samoa, a culture free of the discontinuities that result from fluctuations in creative functioning, the development curve for originality continues a gradual upward trend. The dependent, generally suppressive, culture of Samoa, however, is not generally conducive to creative development.

KAREN, A SIXTH GRADER

Karen stood at the top of the girls in her class on the group-administered test of creative thinking. When I conducted the experiment on heterogeneous grouping, using the science toys, Karen entered into the proceedings with enthusiasm. She soon noted, however, that her dominance of the situation was not appreciated by the other members of the group. Almost immediately, she began to clown and play about, making no contribution to the group goal. One of the boys then assumed the leadership of the group. He was unable to draw Karen back into active participation. When asked for a contribution, she remarked, "I'm a girl. I'm not supposed to know anything about science things like that!"

Earlier, in our development of the Product Improvement Test, we had learned that we had to select toys that were without sex taint. This was especially crucial in the first grade. Many boys refused altogether to make suggestions for the improvement of the nurse's kit or changed it first to a doctor's kit and worked with it on their own terms. Here was another area in which it was taboo for children to permit themselves to think, another area of experience blocked off, made unavailable. The tendency was even more pronounced in the fourth and fifth grades. At the time, in the spring of 1959, about a year and a half after the first Sputnik, public interest in science was rising. We discussed the results of our experiment with both parents and teachers in this particular school and were quite surprised on returning thirteen months later to find that the reluctance among the girls to deal with science materials had disappeared. The girls rated the science-toy experiment as enjoyable as did the boys. They even performed as well as boys, although thirteen months earlier the boys had produced over twice as many ideas as girls. In this school environment, something had happened to make it more acceptable for girls to be interested in science, to enjoy working with science materials and ideas. One thing remained unchanged, however. The contributions of the girls to the success of the group were still rated by their groups as less important than those of boys. (For an account of this experiment, see pp. 145–151.)

JOSEPH, A SEVENTH GRADER

I have not actually met Joseph in person. I know him only through letters from his parents. I have chosen this thirteen-year-old seventh grade boy for an example because the larger percentage of the letters parents write me concern his age group. Eighty-one per cent of the letters written about the difficulties of "creative" children are about boys. The most frequent ages are thirteen, nine, seventeen, and five, in that order. Each of these ages marks a period of decline in creative thinking abilities on our developmental curve, suggesting some discontinuity that contributes to the difficulties of children in adjusting in our society. The situation described by Joseph's mother is typical:

"Joseph is now thirteen years old and has had a steadily declining academic record that ended in his being retained in the seventh grade this year . . . He has a burning *main* interest in electronics and rocks and believe me, his knowledge and interest in these two subjects is great.

"His teachers, principals, and counselors have told me a confusing variety of things (confusing to me anyway). They all agree he is very bright, very bored (daydreams in class constantly), and very withdrawn though not rebellious. Two teachers have told me the school has destroyed his desire to learn. One teacher told me the school cannot help him because the only 'special cases' they are informed enough to help are the 'slow' children. Another teacher said to me, 'I'll make him work if I have to break his spirit to do it — and ridiculing and shaming him is the only way with children like him . . .' Last spring, the school counselor and principal decided that flunking him was the only way to make him 'buckle down and work or else.' He can't join the different types of science clubs because he doesn't have a B average — to which the principal urged that he take up football and become better rounded.

"So many doors closed! Where is the spirit of educating and *cultivating* the child's *natural* desire to learn — some seed of it is *always* there, to one extent or another!

"Now, I will tell you of the boy *I* know, my son . . . He is an irresponsible scatterbrain — he just can't harness his brain to such unimportant things as taking out the trash when he's hot on the trail of discovering perpetual motion. He *never* daydreams, *loves* to learn, and is always getting books from the library. He is a hard worker; many times he almost collapsed trying to work and experiment late into the night. He has energy enough for ten people. He has an outgoing, bubbling personality and a terrific sense of humor. All this he is at home and in the rest of the world *until* he gets to school.

"He speaks of wanting to go to an 'electric college' but says he'll probably quit school when he's sixteen.

"I feel that he is in a steel box — I think he feels he is too and thinks the only way to be free is to get out by quitting.

"How can doors be opened, can you tell me? Can you advise or suggest *anything* that could help?

"*Please*, don't be too busy to care or answer me. I just don't know where else to turn!"

This account, written by a distressed, perhaps desperate mother, is included among these stories of creative students because the internal consistency rings so true to our own empirical findings, those of Getzels and Jackson (1962), and others. This mother describes behaviors and characteristics that closely resemble those of the inventors and creative discoverers we have studied and those of creative persons in other, far more substantial and rigorous studies. The pattern she describes is repeated in letter after letter from almost every section of the United States. Not only is it repeated by parents, but by high school and college students and adults who identify themselves as being or having once been creative.

CHESTER, A COLLEGE STUDENT

I have chosen Chester for an example rather than one of the college students who have written me, or one who has participated in our own studies, because he illustrates so dramatically the use of other methods than testing for identifying creative students and shows that something can be done to help them, even at the college level.

I became acquainted with Chester through his instructor in industrial design. The instructor caught Chester cheating on an examination, an offense which usually brings ejection from the class, failure for the quarter, or some similar penalty. So clever and ingenious were Chester's methods for cheating, however, that the instructor realized he was dealing with an exceptionally talented mind. Suddenly, it occurred to him that his assignments had called only for reproductive thinking and that he had offered nothing to challenge the unusual talents of students like Chester. Instead of giving Chester a failing grade or expelling him from the class, he began thinking up more and more difficult problems calling for creative thinking. Chester worked as he had never worked before and enjoyed it. At the end of the quarter, Chester's achievement was so far ahead of everyone else's in the class that the instructor felt compelled to award him a grade of A.

Here, we have an example of how the identification of this student's unusual talent required a modification of the teacher's usual definition of desirable behavior. Many people would condemn this teacher's behavior as immoral and irresponsible, and say that relaxed discipline in our colleges is responsible for the moral decay of our society. Although I do not condone cheating, the values I place upon freeing students to achieve their potentialities will not permit me to condemn this teacher. Which would have been more immoral, to fail to punish Chester or to fail to recognize the defects of one's teaching procedures and to take corrective action? In my own opinion, recognizing and accepting one's failure to challenge creative talent and attempting to salvage it require far more moral courage than yielding to the need to punish.

CONCLUSION

These eight creative friends of mine throw some light upon the problem of identifying creative students and show that it is possible to use both test and nontest methods as aids in this process, but that to do so we may have to modify the meanings we attach to certain behaviors. Each is an illustration of what makes creative students different, and I hope that teachers who ponder their stories will be reminded of students they know, who need help and understanding.

These eight stories also picture what is happening to creative students in today's schools — much that is good alongside much that is painfully distressing. I think that many exciting things are going to happen in our schools during the next few years, judging from an analysis of 1200 letters received during the period from November 1 to March 1 about our research in this area. Five hundred and fifteen of the writers requested information or materials relative to tests of creative thinking; 496 requested research information; 158 wrote about their research plans; 102 wrote about some cooperative research project or volunteered their schools or classes for experimental studies; 99 were about my participation in some conference, institute, or symposium; 69 expressed an interest in instructional materials; 43 involved requests or other correspondence in relation to manuscripts for publication in professional journals and other magazines; 20 made inquiries about course offerings on creative thinking, creativity testing, and the like; and 172 offered some expression of their appreciation for our work. From this mass of correspondence, it seems clear to me that important and exciting things are happening even now. What distresses me most is that we need so much retooling — tests of ability, tests of achievement, instructional materials, textbooks, courses for teachers, new concepts in counseling, and the like. Although such work is time-consuming and expensive, and must often be conducted without sufficient resources, I hope that more and more people in education will recognize how desperately it needs to be done; once they have, I am sure they will move forward toward the desired goals.

CULTURAL DISCONTINUITIES AND THE
DEVELOPMENT OF ORIGINALITY

WHEN our staff began to study the development of the creative thinking abilities, first by cross-sectional methods and later by longitudinal ones, we were puzzled by what we discovered. Clearly, the intellectual abilities that we had labeled "creative thinking" did not follow the same course of development as other abilities. For most of our measures of creative thinking, there were distinct periods of decline rather than growth at about ages five, nine, thirteen, and seventeen. We became particularly interested in the decline that appears at about age nine, or the fourth grade, because it is so acute and is accompanied by so many problems of behavior, learning difficulty, delinquency, and personality disturbance.

Many possible explanations were advanced for the decline in creative thinking and creative activities in the fourth grade — physiological changes, increasing peer pressures for conformity, and many others. Knowing that the need for consensual validation and peer approval becomes tremendously important at about age nine, I placed a great deal of confidence in hypotheses in this area. Since anthropologists maintain that the United States has one of the most peer-oriented cultures in the world, we have attempted to test some of our hypotheses by conducting developmental studies in several cultures outside the United States and in segregated Negro schools in the United States. Now that the developmental curves for the creative thinking abilities of some of these cultures are becoming clear, the idea has been thrust upon us that the declines in the creative thinking abilities that occur at about ages five, nine, thirteen, and seventeen are the result of the stresses imposed by cultural discontinuities and are accompanied by personality disturbances.

Using the measures of originality on three nonverbal tasks, I should like to discuss some of our findings and thinking concerning this problem. First, I shall describe briefly the tasks used to measure originality

NOTE: This chapter was originally a paper presented to the National Association of Educators of Gifted Children, Columbus, Ohio, April 26, 1962.

of thinking in these cross-cultural studies. Then, I shall present some of the developmental data, review some of the discontinuities in our society, and discuss them in the light of data from five other cultures.

Three nonverbal and six verbal tasks were used for assessing originality of thinking in the cross-cultural studies. Originality has been defined in terms of statistical infrequency of a response within the given culture. In addition, it was required that responses be relevant to the task, show intellectual strength, and represent some break away from the obvious, the commonplace, and the banal. Each of the tasks had undergone considerable developmental work and had yielded satisfactory evidence of test-retest reliability, validity, and ease of administration. From all of the evidence we were able to obtain, the tasks did not seem to favor one sex over the other or one culture over another.

In each of the cultures studied, approximately 1000 pupils in grades one through six were examined. Native examiners were used in all cultures, instructions were given in the native language of the subjects, and the subjects responded in their preferred language. Responses were then translated by expert linguists and afterwards scored by our own staff. Results of the nonverbal tasks are now available for our United States sample (pupils in a school system having a broad range of talent), Australia, Western Samoa, Germany, India, and a sample from segregated Negro schools in Georgia. In Australia we obtained an urban and a rural sample, both in the western part of the continent. The Western Samoan sample included schools in the larger towns and in the remote villages where white men seldom go. In Germany, the samples were from two different sections of Free Berlin. The samples from India included Moslem, Sikh, Christian, and Hindu schools in New Delhi.

Nonverbal Tasks and Scoring for Originality. The three nonverbal tasks on which the measures of originality are based were described in the preceding paper, "Creative Students in Our Schools Today."

To obtain data for a scoring guide, a tabulation was made of the frequency of responses made by the subjects, separately for each culture. Weights from 0 to 4 were assigned on the basis of statistical frequency: 0, 12 per cent or greater; 1, 5 per cent to 12 per cent; 2, 2 per cent to 5 per cent; 3, ½ per cent to 2 per cent; 4, less than ½ per cent.

Some responses are obvious and unoriginal in all cultures; others are common in two or more cultures; while some are common in only one culture. For example, on the Circles Task the following responses were common or unoriginal in all six of the cultures studied: apple; balloons;

balls; clock; coin; design; earth, moon, sun; eggs in some form; flowers; glasses, spectacles (all except Negro); globe; tree; wheels.

The following responses were unoriginal only in the United States samples: baseball; basketball; basketball hoop; door knob; doughnut (fairly unoriginal in Negro and German samples); holes; hoops; steering wheel; sputnik, satellite.

The following were unoriginal only in the United States and Germany: buttons; clown's face; targets; tires.

Responses scored as unoriginal in Samoa, but original in other cultures, include: boat; bowl; breadfruit; cat; leaf; rabbit.

Common among the responses of the sample from India, the following are unoriginal: eggplant; melon; pomegranate; racket; pitcher; table.

Common among the responses of children from Germany are: butterfly; ice cream cone; rabbit; traffic sign; table.

Unoriginal responses among Australian subjects include: decoration (also in U.S.); light bulb (also in U.S.); game; table ware.

Common among the Negro responses are: cat; goat; grapefruit (also other U.S. samples); ice cream cone; lollipop; pumpkin; scissors.

The developmental curves used in this report were obtained by obtaining the sum of the weighted originality scores for the three nonverbal tasks for each subject and then computing the mean for each task for each sample.

DEVELOPMENTAL CURVES IN OUR CULTURE

The generalized developmental curve that holds for most measures we have devised of the creative thinking abilities (see Figure 7) shows that beginning at age three there is an increase until a peak is reached at about age four and a half. A drop occurs at about age five, at about the time the child enters the kindergarten, and is followed by increases in the first, second, and third grades. At about age nine, near the end of the third grade or at the beginning of the fourth grade, there is a rather severe decrement in almost all the creative thinking abilities. Then comes a period of recovery, especially for girls in the fifth grade. Recovery, however, is largely in fluency, not in originality. Recovery in originality comes largely in the sixth grade. After this, another decrease in the seventh grade is followed by recovery in the eighth and continued growth until a peak is reached in the eleventh grade. After this, there is a leveling off or slight drop near the end of the high school period. Although I have not charted carefully the course of development for the remainder of the educational stages, almost no group studied has thus far exceeded the performance of eleventh graders. Studies of the performance of many subjects under many different natural and experimental conditions suggest that decrements continue to occur during other crises or discontinuities throughout the life span.

It is interesting to note that each of the generalized drops occurs at an age at which the transition from one developmental stage to another begins. Using Harry Stack Sullivan's (1953) conceptualization of the stages of development of interpersonal skills, the drop at about age five occurs at the end of the childhood stage and the beginning of the juvenile stage with its demands for social accommodation, compromise, and acceptance of authorities outside the home. The second drop occurs with the onset of the preadolescent stage with its increased need for consensual validation, peer approval, identification with peers of the same sex, and conformity to peer norms. The third occurs at the onset of early adolescence with its increased anxieties, striving for approval of the opposite sex, and the like, all of which restrict many areas of awareness and impose new demands for conformity.

DEVELOPMENTAL CURVES IN OTHER CULTURES

The shape of the developmental curves for originality in other cultures should help us determine whether the various drops we find in our culture are biologically or culturally determined. The mean originality scores for each grade-level for each of the six cultures is shown in Table 3 and Figure 8.

It will be noted that there are no drops in the developmental curve for the Samoan subjects. The level of originality begins in the first grade at the lowest level of any of the cultures but the growth is continuous from year to year. The second greatest continuity in development is shown by the American Negro sample. A slight drop occurs between the second and third grade but there is considerable growth between the third and fourth grades. Through the fourth grade, German and Australian children seem to show about the same level and pattern of devel-

Table 3. Mean Originality Scores on Nonverbal Tasks for Grades One through Six for Six Cultural Groups

Grade	Australia	U.S. Negro	Germany	India	Samoa	U.S.A.
First	17.37	14.58	19.50	14.88	12.72	22.95
Second	17.19	22.35	16.53	13.59	15.27	28.20
Third	15.24	21.42	15.75	17.64	16.08	30.90
Fourth	20.16	26.07	19.83	15.00	18.60	26.40
Fifth	20.76	...	28.44	20.73	19.53	24.90
Sixth	19.83	...	26.07	24.42	22.50	33.30

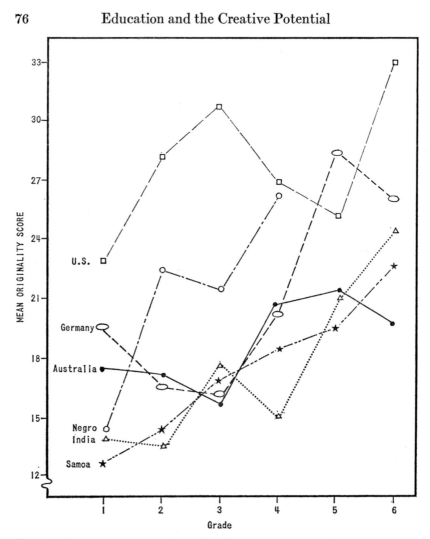

Figure 8. Developmental curve for originality on nonverbal tasks for six cultural groups.

opment. Pressures toward standardization and conformity apparently occur quite early, especially for the Australian child. German children show tremendous growth between the fourth and fifth grades, but the Australian children remain at about the same level in the fourth, fifth, and sixth grades. The pattern of growth among the children in India is much the same as in the United States, though the level is considerably less. (Incidentally, the level of the children in India is comparatively higher on the verbal than on the nonverbal tasks, while the reverse is true of the American Negro sample.)

Now, let us examine some of the evidence concerning the continuities and discontinuities, especially in the United States and Western Samoa, to provide a preliminary test of the hypothesis that cultural discontinuities are accompanied by discontinuities in the development of originality of thinking.

EVIDENCES OF DISCONTINUITY IN OUR CULTURE

Many of the evidences of discontinuity associated with drops in the developmental curves for the creative thinking abilities can be related to the new demands identified in connection with Sullivan's developmental stages, already sketched. A number of others have come to our attention as we have tested school children and observed them in classrooms and playgrounds. A few of these will be reviewed.

Concern about sex appropriateness and emphasis on sex differences become tremendously inhibiting at about age five and continue into the beginning of the first grade. Many children at this age are inhibited in their thinking because they have been harshly warned by parents and teachers to eliminate fantasy. Although we are interested in developing a sound type of creativity, we need to keep fantasy alive until the child's mental development is such that he can engage in realistic creative thinking. Frequently, in individual testing, it has been apparent to me that a child has thought of or repressed an idea. He will smile or grin broadly and begin to speak, only to let the smile change to a pained frown and the eager utterance fade into silence.

We have given more detailed and extended attention to the discontinuities that occur at about age nine when the child reaches the fourth grade. I have discussed this problem with a number of gifted sixth graders, who mention many influences which they feel coerced them to become less imaginative, less curious, and less original in their thinking at about this time. They first point out, "Well, when we went into the fourth grade, we were half through elementary school and they expected us to act more grown up." In the fourth grade they had to begin sitting in orderly rows in the classroom, keeping their feet on the floor. Classroom activity became more organized and formal. Credit was given only for what they put on paper. The animals in their stories did not talk. Usually, they had to go to another building or upstairs in a two-story building. They had to start doing homework and their papers were expected to be neat with no smudges. The subject matter became different; they began having lessons in geography and history. They began taking part in student government and started serving as monitors of their fellow students' behavior.

As we tested children of this age, we were impressed with the inhibiting influence of their preoccupation with prevention and fear of making mental leaps. The problem, "What are all of the possible things Mother Hubbard could have done when she found no bone in the cupboard for her dog?" was easy for younger children but extremely difficult for the nine-year-old. The nine-year-old was so preoccupied with the notion that Old Mother Hubard should have prevented this predicament that he could think of no way she might remedy it. These older children also wanted to stick close to the stimuli and resisted making mental leaps. In the Product Improvement Task resistance in many cases seemed to stem from the inhibitions surrounding cost. Uncertainty expressions became frequent. These phenomena have been observed and documented by other investigators. For example, L'Abate (1957) found that nine-year-olds showed a greater use of uncertainty expressions. Professional workers in the field of remedial vision have also observed uncertainty in children of this age. On the Rorschach test, subjects will say they are less imaginative than other children and that they can't make anything out of the ink blots. They will practice visual-training exercises endlessly but fail to make progress, continuing to be uncertain, hesitant, and slow in their perceptions.

Our work with teachers has also shown that many teachers in the intermediate grades live in a world quite different from that of their colleagues who teach in the primary grades. Their training, their attitudes toward children, and their methods of instruction have little in common. Many intermediate teachers admit frankly that they have no idea about what goes on in the primary grades.

In our research we have also found that primary teachers, when working with the creative writing of children, were more willing than intermediate teachers to sacrifice preoccupation with correctness and form for creative values.

When a youngster enters the seventh grade, he usually has to go to another building, frequently in another part of town, in a strange neighborhood. The school is usually larger, with different teachers for each subject. Promptness is strongly emphasized and tardy slips impose penalties. Extremes in dress and appearance, deviations from what all the others are wearing, are discouraged. New pressures and anxieties arise about winning the approval of the opposite sex. Pressures to be well-rounded socially and athletically are intensified.

Apparently the transition from junior high school is marked by greater continuity than that from elementary school. Since our developmental data are based on samples from schools having both junior and senior high schools in the same building, with a continuous organization, this aspect of continuity-discontinuity may be operating. Our data suggest that some discontinuities are introduced into the senior high school about the senior year and may be attributed to the immediacy of the transition to college, work, or military service at that time. New demands for grown-up behavior and sanctions against regression to childish thinking are then being experienced.

INDICATIONS OF PERSONALITY DISTURBANCE IN OUR CULTURE

A recent experience has strongly reinforced my observation that considerable personality disturbance is associated with the stresses of discontinuity at about ages five, nine, thirteen, and seventeen. I analyzed a sample of one hundred letters written to me by parents whose children fell into some kind of trouble because of their creativity. Figure 9 presents the data derived from this analysis. The greatest frequency of letters corresponds with the drops in the developmental curves, giving a rough indication that many creative children are in trouble at each of these stages. From these data it would seem that parents most frequently tend to be disturbed about their nine- and thirteen-year-olds. The five- and the seventeen-year-olds cause the next greatest concern.

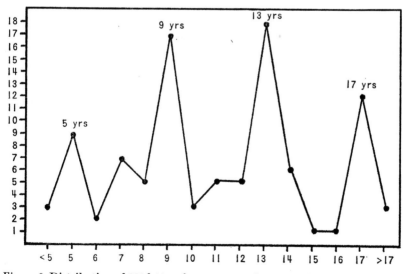

Figure 9. Distribution of 100 letters from parents about creative children in difficulty, according to age.

For each of these age groups, the following excerpts from the letters illustrate the nature of these personality disturbances.

Age Five

"In January, the head of the school recommended that Don be removed from school because of his inability to conform."

"Upon arriving at public school, John clung to me and cried bitterly. He was taken day after day and he remained. His interest span remained short and his hyperactivity persisted."

"To make Carl remain in his chair, his teacher used rope to tie him. A school conference revealed the teacher's opinion that he was heading for the life of a criminal. It was during this period that he reverted to soiling his pants."

One type of school experimentation now growing in popularity is introducing a discontinuity in the first grade, which apparently is associated with personality disturbance for some children and apparent losses in creativity, as described by one mother:

"Charles is in one of the few schools to adopt a new plan of education. He moves from room to room for different subjects. It's sponsored by the local college. His desire to have the teacher single him out if only to scold him makes me wonder if this plan is making him feel insecure. One teacher that Charles likes told me that he asks directions to the next class every few minutes. He is constantly at her side."

Age Nine

"Each year since the first grade, the teachers have raved about Ray's creative ability, but moaned over his reading development. This year (his fourth in school) has been the first that he hasn't been in the bottom group, but also, since he's learned to conform, his creativity is not as outstanding as formerly. He tries not to be different, he says!"

"When Tom was about nine, his teacher was an older woman who returned to teaching after eleven years away from the classroom. His demand for attention resulted in his confinement in the hall coat room. He took off. He had his special hiding places around the neighborhood, and the school would phone me to come up. The principal, gym teacher, and I would hunt for him. He was usually found fairly easily by me."

"Asked outright, the school replied that they admit defeat, that they haven't been able to reach Bruce . . . asked for specific diagnosis, with reference to the broad term, 'Emotionally Disturbed,' the specific is 'Behavioral Disturbance.' They say he is not retarded and that he is not psychotic."

"In the fourth grade, George had a disastrous year. He had a rigid teacher who tried to bend him to his will and he would not comply. Needless to say, the war was on . . . After this sad experience, we sent him to a creative art camp during the summer where he bloomed like a filly kicking up its heels at being free. He did some marvelous work."

Age Thirteen

"When Jerry gets up to make an unorthodox statement he is ridiculed and so I find him becoming more and more introverted. He travels alone though he loves companionship but the boys his age don't know what he is talking about. He prefers the company of men with his interests."

"In the first grade Bob was a happy child who wanted to go to school more than anything . . . And even before he started to school, several friends had noted his unusual questions and answers and asked if he was in the third or fourth grade . . . But today his disposition has changed. He is still a happy boy and a ball of energy when he has time and is left alone to create something seemingly senseless to the adults around him . . . Is he mentally retarded? I cannot believe it." *

Age Seventeen

Many in this group have already left school or are in the process of leaving. School proved to be unchallenging or they were unable in some way to conform to its requirements. Some are described as lonely and mixed up, confused. Others had been unwilling to conform during the first few years of high school but had started making all A's, although their grade-point averages are still so low that they will have difficulty gaining admission to a "respectable" college. Their parents are concerned that these youngsters will not be able to earn a living and will have difficulty surviving.

One seventeen-year-old girl wrote that she no longer considers herself a creative person. During the first two years of high school, she expressed her opinions and ideas and held to the truth as she saw it. As a consequence, she was ridiculed, laughed at, scorned, and given low grades. She then decided that she would keep quiet in class and began to earn A's. She now feels that she has cheated herself. Her over-all high school average is mediocre, in spite of the high grades earned during the past two years. Furthermore, she feels that she has become less of a person in adopting conformity and surrendering her independence of

* See also the letter by a mother of a thirteen-year-old boy on p. 69, which vividly describes the difficulties of a creative youngster at this age.

mind. She feels that she has not taken the courageous course. Boys who have adopted conformity have even greater feelings of guilt, perhaps, and consider themselves effeminate to have given in.

CONTINUITIES AND DISCONTINUITIES IN OTHER CULTURES

Since the development of originality of thinking shows greater con-tinuity in Western Samoa than in any of the other cultures studied, it seems desirable to examine the Samoan data in considerable detail. Margaret Mead's pioneering work (1939), the reports of modern ob-servers (Johnson, 1962), and the data of this study support a picture of high cultural continuity and suppression of creativity and independ-ence of thought almost from birth.

According to Margaret Mead, "Keep still," "Sit still," "Keep your mouth shut," and "Stop that noise," are thoroughly ingrained into the Samoan child. He is not even permitted to cry. Since the older children are given responsibility for disciplining the younger ones, conformity is taught from birth. Even today, Samoan teachers place an unusually high value upon *quietness* as a desirable characteristic on our "Ideal Pupil Questionnaire." Mead pointed out that Samoans were imitative and reproductive in their crafts rather than creative. Likewise, today we find that Samoan children excel in the craftsmanship of their draw-ings, when administered the Goodenough Human Drawing Test or Buck's House-Tree-Person Test. Their drawings are reproductive rather than creative. The characteristic most valued by Samoan teachers in their pupils is *remembering well.*

Mead and other observers stress the role of the extended family, the participation of all ages in the life of the community, and the mixing of all ages in Samoa. Mead uses these facts and the continuities in regard to sex in explaining why Samoan adolescents do not experience the periods of emotional upset and personality disturbances common among adolescents in the United States. In today's Samoan schools there is no strict age segregation and a wide range of ages is found in a single grade, especially in the remote government schools.

The following three characteristics were ranked highest by Samoan teachers on the Ideal Pupil Checklist: remembers well, is healthy, and is always asking questions. From other data, it is obvious that "always ask-ing questions" means something quite different to the Samoan teacher as opposed to the United States teacher. It was even difficult to admin-ister the test of creative thinking to Samoan pupils, because they con-tinually asked, "Is this all right?" "Is this what you want?" Samoan teachers tended to rank the following characteristics *lower* than the teachers of other cultures: adventurous, a self-starter, curious, determined, energetic, independent in judgment, industrious, self-confident, self-sufficient, sincere, thorough, and versatile. They tended to place a *higher* value than teachers in other cultures on being a good guesser, competitive, prompt, haughty, physically strong, quiet, and liking to work alone. In general, this pattern of values is likely to support cultural continuity and a low degree of creativity.

Johnson (1962), who directed collection of the data in Western Samoa, identifies three major factors underlying this pattern. First, conformity is deeply embedded in thousands of years of Samoan history. A strong patriarchal family system evolved with emphasis on a chain of command, the highest decisions being made in the village "fono" of chiefs and passed down to submissive subjects. Acceptance of authority relationships was apparently rewarded and regarded as an ideal characteristic. A second influence is attributed to the influx of missionaries and German traders since the early 1830's. Here also the emphasis was on submission, either to God and his "special representatives," or to the traders who needed submissive workers on the plantations. A third influence began with New Zealand's entrance into the government of Samoa in 1914. With this came the idea of an extensive school system, school uniforms, leaving examinations, and uniformity of learning.

Both in the government and in the schools the authoritarian, hierarchal traditions were extended. In other ways, however, the schools introduced by the New Zealanders do not reflect the culture of the people. This is apparently more evident in the remote areas of the island where government educators inspect the schools regularly but are the only contact the people have with the "palagis" (whites). The school is modified somewhat but the culture of the village hardly changes.

Johnson cites the example of Faleolo to show how thoroughly students are imbued with the attitude of doing nothing until told. Faleolo, the housegirl of one of the teachers, satisfactorily performed the tasks assigned her. When the teacher returned from a two-day trip, he discovered that the girl had not eaten during the entire time. When he asked her why, she replied, "You didn't tell me to eat." In the Samoan home, children are told each thing they are to do.

Johnson also remarks upon the excellent memory of Samoan children today. Memory is important in the leaving examinations stressed in the school system. (One question in the 1960 examination: "How many eggs does an earthworm lay in a season?") Mead, about thirty years ago, observed that Samoans were notorious for their poor memory. Although this emphasis on memory for the great mass of Samoan children may have come with the mission and government schools, memory has long been important to Samoan rulers. Written language is a recent innovation in Samoa. Samoan leaders always had to memorize tapa designs, history, legends, songs, and rituals.

It is interesting to note that along with the importance attached to remembering, Samoan teachers regard a "good guesser" with high favor. Johnson relates that on occasion he has written a mathematical formula on the blackboard, had students work out a proof, asked a question about the formula that would necessitate an obvious "no" answer, given deliberate yet subtle "yes" cues with his head, and received incorrect "yes" answers by almost everyone in the class.

Apparently, a number of discontinuities are creeping into Samoan culture, in the more urban mission schools. Many of the Christian taboos are contrary to the traditions of the culture. Johnson recounts one incident in which two adolescent boys came to him as a counselor, requesting that a certain girl be expelled. Johnson recognized the accused girl as one of the school's leading students and a model of circumspect behavior. Puzzled, he sought to learn the reason for the boys' request. They explained simply that whenever they touched her she hit them, behavior approved by the school but disapproved by the culture and upsetting to the cultural continuity governing sex relationships.

These emerging discontinuities are reflected in the development curves, if we separate the more urban mission schools from the more remote government schools. The resulting developmental curves are shown in Figure 10. Although the degree of originality is lower in the more remote schools, there is no break in the continuity of development. The introduction of discontinuities seems to be associated with a rise in the level of originality, discontinuity in the development of originality, and personality conflict. In Western Samoa the problem of increasing originality in thinking seems to be one of how to introduce cultural discontinuities without producing undue personality conflicts and disruptions in the development of thinking abilities. In the United States the problem seems to be the reverse: how to reduce the cultural discontinuities without retarding creative development.

Although the limitations of this paper do not permit an examination of the data from India, Australia, and Germany, and from American Negroes, it can be stated that thus far the results are in harmony with what has been presented here. The data from India are especially interesting. No break was found in the developmental curve for the sample from an orthodox Sikh school, yet the general level of originality is lower than in any of the other six schools in the sample from India. The

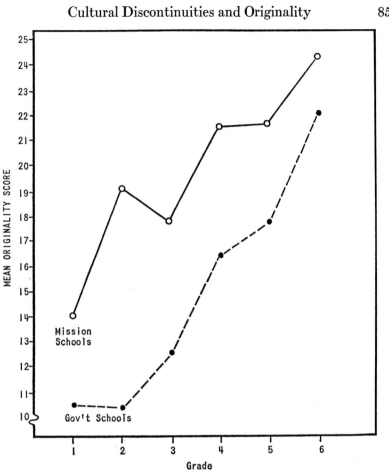

Figure 10. Developmental curve for originality on nonverbal tasks for remote government schools and more urban mission schools.

two Indian schools in which there is greatest discontinuity in the development of originality are characterized by the diversity of their pupils. Both are coeducational and enroll children from different religious, linguistic, and socioeconomic backgrounds.

REDUCING THE DISCONTINUITIES IN AMERICAN EDUCATION

As I have explored with imaginative, creative teachers the problems associated with the drops in creative thinking ability at various ages, I have found that many teachers have devised ways for reducing the discontinuities. Frequently, however, they have had to violate school rules and policies in order to carry out these procedures. The following absorbing account written by a teacher of "beginners" illustrates many of the problems associated with the reduction of discontinuities among school children in the United States:

"Of the twenty children who will be starting the first grade, none has been in kindergarten. Some of them will have trouble adjusting to school, but they will have to understand that they are big boys and girls now. There will be no babying and positively no mothers." This was the principal speaking at a preschool teachers' meeting.

At eight o'clock in the morning of the fourth day of school after the opening of the fall term, Miss Ellis was at her desk, trying to straighten out her plans for the day, before the onslaught of commotion that would announce the arrival of her forty-six pupils, grades one, two, and three. The principal's words rang in her ears. In her room there was work enough for two teachers. How could she handle it alone? And then there was the problem of Jimmy. There always had to be at least one beginner who had trouble "settling in." Would he be like Margie of a previous year who became ill several times a week? On every such occasion her mother had had to be called to take her home. When her mother arrived, Margie always sobbed, "I was so lonesome for you, Mommy," but no one could deny that the child was sick. Her violently upset stomach gave evidence of that. Now there was Jimmy. Would the stress of his first days of school be too great for him, too? The first two days, he had simply followed his sister to her eighth grade room. There he had been forcibly separated from his sister by the principal and had been carried, kicking and screaming, down the corridor to his own room where he sat, crying and trembling, until time for dismissal. Yesterday he had deliberately missed the bus.

The bell rang, and as the children trooped in, Miss Ellis had a fleeting hope that the fire-inspector — or somebody — would decide that she had too many children — or, at least, that a kind angel would solve the problem of Jimmy. Looking over the sea of faces, she noticed that, once again, Jimmy was not there.

Nevertheless, there was no time to worry. First things first — the Pledge of Allegiance and a verse of the "Star Spangled Banner"; but the Pledge of Allegiance was barely finished when came a rap on the door. It was Jimmy *and* his mother. Both looked a little frightened. "Do you mind if I stay?" whispered Mrs. Lon. "I know it is against the rules but I thought I might help."

"I shall be very glad to have you stay," Miss Ellis replied, and then mentally clapped a hand over her mouth. "What have I said? Now I have broken a rule." However, the words were out, and as the day wore on, she had no feeling of regret. Somehow, everything was going better. Mrs. Lon circulated throughout the room, helping all the children. She paid no particular attention to Jimmy, nor he to her. During intermission he went out to play with the other children and immediately found a "special" friend. When Miss Ellis met the principal in the corridor at noon, he said, "What? A mother already?" She replied, "Yes, and I am so very glad to have her."

Mrs. Lon was in school again the next day. She was very unobtrusive and, somehow, the children gathered that she was there to help their teacher. So ended the first week of school. Thereafter, Jimmy needed no further help in adjusting to his new role. He was a happy child and a good student. As for Miss Ellis, she could not help thinking that the unorthodox procedure may not always work, but that it did this time, and that she might try it again sometime! She felt rather pleased about having been able to alleviate Mrs. Lon's feeling of guilt for being where she knew the head of the school did not want her: "I was deeply wishing for a kind angel to help me with my problems."

Essentially what this teacher did was to reduce in a small degree the discontinuity between home and the beginning of school for Jimmy. Perhaps there are many other ways by which this could have been done, but this case illustrates a number of the problems involved in reducing cultural discontinuities.

One important problem not answered by this case is that of determining whether or not the reduction in cultural discontinuities will reduce the drop observed in the creative thinking abilities as measured by our tests. Positive clues concerning this issue, however, were obtained from studies of the creative development of the pupils of two fourth grade teachers in our project. The pupils of these two teachers did not experience a decline in their creative development during this period. In both cases, the teacher did many things to reduce the discontinuities and their stressfulness. One of them permitted his pupils to continue experimenting in the fourth grade with different seating arrangements, as they had done in the third grade. He did not insist that they sit in rigid rows with their feet flat on the floor. He kept them writing poems, stories, and plays, and their inventions continued to have a place in the classroom. These activities were so exciting that the instructor did not have to make his pupils waste time in writing five hundred times, "I will not whisper in German class" or "I will not run in the hall." Along with their continued creative development, the children also experienced more than the usual growth in reading, language, study skills, and arithmetic. Similar observations could be made about the second teacher and his efforts to encourage creativity.

If we are able to establish more firmly that some of our cultural discontinuities are associated with personality disorganization and decreased mental functioning in certain areas and that some of these discontinuities are unnecessary, imaginative teachers, curriculum workers, and administrators should be able to devise changes, and evaluate the effects of changes, that will reduce these discontinuities.

RELIGIOUS EDUCATION AND CREATIVE THINKING

MAN's natural inclination is to learn creatively. By learning creatively he acquires much of his really useful knowledge. By learning creatively he acquires his enduring beliefs. God has commanded man to live creatively. Yet in education we have traditionally insisted that man acquire his *knowledge* from authority. In religious education we have usually insisted that he acquire his *beliefs* from authority.

In a way it is strange that Christian educators have insisted upon teaching largely by authority, since Jesus himself was such a good example of the creative learner and the creative teacher. The first picture we have of Jesus after his birth and infancy shows him asking questions —one of the basic techniques for learning creatively. At the age of twelve, when left behind in Jerusalem by his parents, he was found in the Temple "sitting among the teachers, listening to them, and asking them questions" (Luke 2.46). Jesus' inquiring tendency seems to have stayed with him throughout his life, as it does with all really creative teachers. According to Price (1946, pp. 110–111), the Scriptures record 154 questions asked by Jesus. Another source maintains that more than a hundred different questions by Jesus are scattered among the four gospels.

As a teacher, Jesus also aroused the curiosity of others. People asked him many questions. He always treated their questions with respect and helped them find the answers. Of course, he may have answered their questions by asking them several of his own, to make them think. Jesus recognized thoroughly and acted upon the old law of teaching: "Excite and direct the self-activities of the learner, and tell him nothing he can learn for himself (Gregory, 1886, p. 82). Instead of giving ready-made solutions Jesus threw people back on their own resources. Habitually he would throw in a question now and then that broke up the serenity of his pupils and made them sit up and think.

NOTE: This chapter was originally a paper presented at the Institute on Creativity in Religious Education, Center for Continuation Study, University of Minnesota, October 25, 1960.

Today we have available a variety of definitions for creativity. In our own work which has been concerned with the kinds of thinking which are involved in creative achievements, we have chosen to define creative thinking as a process — the process of sensing gaps or needed missing elements; of forming ideas or hypotheses concerning them; of testing these hypotheses; and of communicating the results, possibly modifying and retesting the hypotheses. Under this definition we have been quite willing to subsume the major features of other definitions that have been proposed. Included in most of these definitions is "the production of something new." Another commonly employed defining term is "adventurous thinking"— getting away from the main track, breaking out of the mold, being open to experience, and permitting one thing to lead to another. Creative thinking has also been defined as the initiative manifested by one's ability to break away from the usual sequence of thought into an altogether different but productive sequence. Above all, creative thought must be "true."

The criterion "it must be true" is as important in religious education as it is in science. Many a scientist has missed making an important discovery in the natural world, or in the social world, because he was biased before he started as to what he wanted to find. He was not willing to discover the world as it actually is. At this point I should like to emphasize, however, that I do not limit my use of creativity to apply only to that original creativity signified by the scientific discoverer, the inventor, the creative artist, or the composer. In order to be spiritually creative a person must be able to participate meaningfully in life and by so doing change that in which he participates, even if only in small ways.

The Christian's real duty is to live creatively. We are taught that we were made "in the image and likeness of God," and when we create we are to some extent exercising that God-like quality within us. It gives us a feeling of contentment and satisfaction. To groups of educators, I have frequently asserted that the greatest reward a child achieves for learning, is doing something with what he has learned, using it to think and to behave creatively.

THE VALUE OF CREATIVE THINKING

Almost every phase of life activity today is in dire need of creative people — people with vision, people with originality and initiative. The world is constantly paying large premiums to those who can invent a new idea, a new device, a new way to make something. This does not mean that new ideas are generally welcomed; many of the greatest ideas have been at least temporarily spurned and their initiators dishonored. Such people are important, however, to the very survival of the human race. We need a large number of people who can and will face facts, no matter how uncomfortable and threatening; who will think and act independently of past attitudes and in terms of the world as it is now.

In the past the importance of creative thinking has been given considerable recognition in many areas of life. We have recognized its importance in mental health and personality adjustment. We have recognized creativity as an essential characteristic of all truly outstanding men and women. We have long recognized that high intelligence, special abilities, and outstanding technical skills together are not enough. We have even recognized the importance of creative thinking in coping with difficult and stressful problems of everyday life.

When it comes to learning, however, we have generally assumed, or acted as though we assumed, that it is better to teach altogether or primarily by authority rather than creatively. A number of recent breakthroughs by research in education and psychology are rapidly changing this view, notably the work of Guilford and his associates on the identification and measurement of the creative thinking abilities. One of the first of these breakthroughs, a study by Getzels and Jackson (1962), at the University of Chicago, impressively demonstrated that the creative thinking abilities are useful in acquiring knowledge. Since that time, we have completed here at the University of Minnesota eight partial replications of the Getzels-Jackson study in different situations.

Getzels and Jackson administered a battery of creative thinking tests to all the pupils enrolled in one high school, a university laboratory school. They separated into one group pupils ranking in the upper 20 per cent on traditional measures of intelligence (IQ tests) but not in the upper 20 per cent on measures of creativity. In the other group they placed those who ranked in the upper 20 per cent on creativity but not on IQ. They then compared the achievement of these two groups of adolescents as measured by standardized achievement tests in the subjects they had taken, not on teachers' grades. In spite of an average difference of 23 IQ points between these two groups, there was no difference in their measured achievement. What little difference existed was in favor of the high creatives. The teachers, however, expressed a definite preference for the high IQ pupils.

Five of our replications of the Getzels-Jackson study were at the elementary school level, one at the high school level, and two at the adult or graduate level. Six of these eight replications yielded results almost identical to those obtained by Getzels and Jackson. The two exceptions were at the elementary school level, one in a school conducted by a religious organization and one in a small-town school. Even in these schools, however, a significant relationship between measures of creativity and measures of achievement emerged. Furthermore, considerable over-achievement among the highly creative was evident — that is, if one judges over-achievement on the basis of IQ. For example, the average IQ of the highly creatives in the small-town school was 98, but their achievement quotient averaged 122.

The situation in the school in which we first replicated the study is significant. Although we obtained an average difference in IQ of over 25 points, certainly a big enough difference to cause us to expect a difference in achievement, no statistically significant differences emerged. Such learnings as reading and language skills favored the creatives; study-work skills and arithmetic skills favored the high IQ children. The teachers preferred as pupils the high IQ children, saying they knew these children better and that they were more ambitious, hard-working, and studious. How, then, did the high creatives manage to achieve as well as the high IQ children, if they in addition to being 25 points lower on IQ are also less ambitious, less studious, and less hard-working? My answer is that they acquire much of what they learn through creativeness rather than by authority. They learn by asking questions, by inquiring and exploring. To the adult, it may look as if they are wasting time in pointless activity, but this is the way they learn.

Seldom are adults willing to permit children to follow their curiosity, letting one thing lead to another. Almost never have we contrived situations in which children are impelled by curiosity to go on learning over an extended period of time. We catch a glimpse of the possibilities here in the experiments of O. K. Moore (1961) in teaching preschool children to read and write. Because he found that small children are curious about typewriters, especially electric typewriters, Professor Moore's preschoolers start with the free exploration of the electric typewriter. Impelled by their curiosity, they are permitted to operate the machines freely, the experimenter not directing them but responding only to their questions. These children soon learn how the letters look and find that in their scribbling they can make letters like the ones they type. In the same way, they soon learn to read, spell, and punctuate at what appears to a phenomenal level.

Both of these experiences effectively demonstrate that children can learn many things creatively, perhaps more economically than they can learn by authority.

People may tell me that creative thinking applies only to intellectual skills and has no bearing upon beliefs, and that in religious education we are interested in a man's beliefs, his faith. What do we know about how we learn or acquire our beliefs?

It is well known that a little child will believe in the existence of fairyland, Santa Claus, and the big bad wolf, if stories about these are told to him. Christian beliefs can be taught in the same way. In some degree the establishment of such beliefs might be owing to the child's submission to the authority of the storyteller. They will not become enduring beliefs, however, unless impulses other than submission to authority are at work.

Childhood beliefs taught by authority alone endure only for a few years. How are they corrected, abandoned, or reinforced and confirmed? Again, authoritative suggestion, hostile to the reality of the thing believed, might break down the belief, or, if friendly, confirm it for a time. Confirmation by authority will not endure, however, unless the belief is confirmed by creative participation, unless the belief is tested by experience. It is the impulse of curiosity that leads to this kind of learning. But we have many ways of discouraging the child who exhibits curiosity. We ridicule his questions, we rebuff them as signs of "mere idle curiosity." In the Sunday School class taught by authority, the child soon learns that there are certain questions — frequently the ones most vital to Christian belief — that one just doesn't ask. Soon he is afraid to ask any questions at all, and the teacher has lost his most powerful force for motivating learning — helping the child find the answers to his questions.

What do we know about changing human behavior and personality? We know that to persuade men that they ought to do something has at best only a temporary effect. To change one's personality requires more than a firm decision to be a different man in the future. Personality is changed very little, if at all, by logical reasoning. The futility of a disintegrating emotional appeal is well known. We know that many things in our programs of religious education can be used as the vehicles for changing personality. Whatever these are, the individual must experience them creatively — he must be conscious of their meaning, throw himself into their spirit, and think himself into them.

KINDS OF CREATIVE THINKING

Most of what we know about the creative thinking abilities has grown out of work related to expanding our concepts of man's thinking abilities. Guilford and his associates at the University of Southern California have devised an interesting new way of classifying these thinking abilities (Guilford and Merrifield, 1960). Their theoretical model of the "Structure of Intellect" provides us with something analogous to Mendeléev's periodic table in chemistry. According to this model there are 120 mental abilities. Thus far, about fifty-six have been identified. Five mental operations are applied to three kinds of content and six kinds of products.

A look at these mental operations is necessary in order to grasp something of the nature of the creative thinking abilities and the difference between these abilities and those sampled by traditional measures of intelligence. First, we have the cognitive operations, involved in recognizing, becoming aware of, and the like. Second, we have memory, which comes into play in retaining what has been cognized. Next, we have two kinds of productive thinking used in producing something new from what has been cognized and memorized. Divergent thinking is involved when possible solutions are many, whereas convergent thinking proceeds toward a restricted answer or solution — the only correct answer, the one accepted or approved solution. Finally, the evaluative abilities are involved when we assess what has been cognized, memorized, and produced, to determine its correctness, suitability, or adequacy.

Originally, it was thought that the thinking abilities involved in creativity were those defined as divergent productions and transformations. Recent research, however, has shown that creative thinking also includes the redefinition abilities, which are in the convergent-production category, and sensitivity to problems, in the evaluation category.

Sensitivity to Problems. Sensitivity to problems, as we have defined it, is the ability to see defects, needs, and deficiencies, to see the odd and the unusual, to see what needs to be done. At this level, I believe that most clergymen and church leaders would agree that they would like to see the people in their churches develop this ability to a high degree. Practically, however, I suspect that they would be quite intolerant of any church member who *actually* did much of this kind of thinking in connection with the church's educational program.

When one is sensitive to problems, he starts asking questions; but, as I have already indicated, we are adept at silencing the questioning child or adult. We grant no respect to the questions asked. We call them "silly, absurd, or crazy." We tell the questioner that he should know better: "You mean that you don't know that," "So you think you know more than the book," or "I can't teach you anything, if you don't believe what the lesson says." We ignore questions or try to answer them without knowing the answers ourselves.

Ill-prepared Sunday School teachers are likely to feel sorely pressed by children's questions. Religious educators need to help them find the courage to admit their ignorance when they have no answer. Since we generally teach by authority, however, it is difficult for the average Sunday School teacher to reveal that his knowledge is limited. In my opinion, it would be far better for the teacher to admit without hesitation that he does not know *the* answer to a question than to cover himself with hypocrisy. Children sense a teacher's evasiveness or untruthfulness and lose faith in him accordingly. Evading an issue or giving erroneous answers only weakens his authority.

My real fear, however, is that the child's impulse to question may be smothered in the beginning. In most programs of religious education children learn too early that "you just don't question religious ideas." Unless children are given a chance to think by being allowed to question and doubt and test and prove, they will cease to think. They will come to accept what is handed down to them from above and become slaves to learning by authority, muddling along without thought or care.

Questioning is thinking; so long as a mind questions honestly, it grows in understanding. One must think in order to create, and thinking feeds on questions. So long as a question prods him on, the child will strive with might and main toward his answer, and in answering use his creative power.

One mark of the person who lives creatively is that he always has some thorn in his flesh. Always bothered by some problem, always aware of some defect, some need, some deficiency, he is concerned about finding remedies and solutions.

Ideational Fluency. One of the abilities most needed now is ideational fluency, the ability to produce a variety of ideas or hypotheses concerning possible solutions to problems. In an earlier stage of our research, my associates and I demonstrated in a number of situations that groups find better solutions when there is a tolerance for divergence of ideas (Torrance, 1957). Even in making estimates for a given problem, we obtain greater accuracy when a wider range of possibilities is considered.

Two of the test tasks we use in measuring ideational fluency provide examples of how this ability may be developed through religious education and how it can be used to make religious teachings more meaningful. In one task we ask the subjects to think of all of the possible consequences of a particular state of affairs. Usually we posit an improbable situation: "What would happen if a hole were bored through the earth?" "What would happen if men could fly without mechanical aids?" Children need to be taught to use their imaginations to think through the consequences of their behavior. Problems of this kind can be used fruit-fully in almost any Sunday School lesson. A simple prototype is "What would happen if you practiced the Golden Rule?"—or any other religious precept?

In another problem designed to stimulate ideational fluency, we ask the subjects to think of all the possible uses they can for bricks or tin cans or the like. In the graduate courses I teach, I give my students a research finding or a well-established principle and ask them to think of all of the uses they can for this finding or principle in their professional careers, in education, and elsewhere. Almost any Sunday School lesson has infinite possibilities for this kind of exploitation. The lessons we seek to teach are likely to have little impact until we stimulate our pupils to do this kind of thinking.

Flexibility. Another important ability involved at this stage of creative thinking is flexibility, the ability to adapt to changing instructions, to be free from inertia of thought, to use a variety of approaches. Their flexibility is one of the reasons why children sometimes come up with such brilliant solutions to problems or see the truth so plainly when others are blind to it. The fable of the king who wore no clothes is a striking example of this phenomenon. Such insights were at work in Jesus' teachings when he warned, "except ye become as a little Child, ye cannot enter the Kingdom of Heaven." Our tests show that children tend to be more flexible than adults and that mentally healthy adults are more flexible than unhealthy ones. For example, in the task which requires the subject to suggest possible uses for tin cans, 17 per cent of responses from the fourth, fifth, and sixth grades are container responses—but these children put such interesting things in tin cans. Among healthy adults (college students), 37 per cent of the uses listed are container responses, and the things they put in tin cans are far less interesting. Among schizophrenics on the road to recovery we found 87 per cent container responses, and the things they suggested putting in tin cans are positively boring—nothing more imaginative than soups and vegetables.

Many people may object to the idea of looking at the Scriptures from different approaches and considering alternative interpretations. I suspect, however, that we could increase our understanding of the Scriptures and develop more accurate, more realistic beliefs, if more thinking of this kind went on in religious education.

Originality. Originality is the ability to produce uncommon responses; remote, unusual, or unconventional associations; cleverness. Originality is perhaps the most striking aspect of creative thinking as well as the most upsetting, most threatening, most discomforting. Originality invites the strongest sanctions from society, the strongest taboos in religious education. Although I respect high standards of excellence, I am at times provoked when good ideas are vetoed or silenced by, "We won't meet the Standard of Excellence if we do it that way." I think every enterprise in religious education would do well to take stock of its multitude of blocks to originality and take up the challenge to produce better ideas for getting the Lord's work done.

We underrate the ability to do original thinking because we overrate the finished product — the finished poem, the finished song, the polished sermon. Deceived by its comparative smoothness, we evaluate the finished product as if it were the immediate delivery of a creative act. Even the Sermon on the Mount was perhaps first a burning, spontaneous, creative matrix, long before it became the beautifully polished sermon which every minister can repeat (Moreno, 1947).

Penetration. Failure to penetrate, to get underneath the problem, to get away from the obvious, failure to work creative thinking into religious education programs is, I believe, one of the major reasons why we fail to hold people and to keep them interested. We keep giving them only the obvious, failing to think creatively ourselves, and failing to stimulate this kind of thinking in our participants.

Analysis and Synthesis. Interpretation of the Scriptures relies upon analysis in trying to puzzle out meanings more completely, more deeply. And the ideas produced by analysis, no matter how original or penetrating, must be synthesized or organized into some meaningful order that shows "what it all adds up to."

Redefinition. Finally, the ability to redefine, to reorganize what we see in new ways, to shift the function of a familiar object, to see something well known in a new context, is the transformation that makes thinking productive rather than reproductive. A number of studies have shown that much classroom teaching inhibits children's thinking by forcing them to do what they are told, rather than what they think a problem calls for. These children learn to work by textbook and by rule, reproductively rather than constructively.

Frequently creativity involves a change in use, or even the destruction of what is present — a child's toy, perhaps — out of which something new is developed. Attention is focused so intensively on the new need, the new demand, that the object worked upon has to be changed, transformed, or even destroyed to produce the new. I suspect this is what prompted Jesus to tell Nicodemus that he must be "born again," that he must destroy the old, that he must become as a new-born babe so that he can really grow up, so that he can live creatively. I suspect this is what motivated Paul to beseech the Romans to "be not conformed to this world: but be ye transformed by the renewing of your mind, that ye may prove what *is* that good, and acceptable, and perfect, will of God." (Romans 12.2.)

JESUS AS A CREATIVE LEARNER AND TEACHER

If we re-examine the life and teachings of Jesus, we find in him a good model of the creative learner and teacher. We find that he was himself continually engaging in the kinds of thinking that I have sketched briefly, and stimulating his pupils to do likewise.

Jesus is a good example of the teacher who stimulates his pupils to use their knowledge to think. He had a way of getting straight at the important issues. He did not teach the rudiments of learning, nor the history, geography, and customs of Palestine. Nor do we find in his teaching much emphasis on organization, equipment, and materials. He set forth no elaborate system of doctrine to be drilled into future generations. His nearest approach to doctrine is the Sermon on the Mount. He did not even stress the memorization of Scripture, though he certainly had at his command for creative use a great deal of Scripture. He did not spend his time merely in denouncing the issues of the day. His was not merely a gospel of "quit your meanness." Rather he recognized the necessity of a positive, creative approach. He tried to show the covetous inheritor that life is more than possessions, and the sordid Samaritan woman that there are higher satisfactions than the physical. He was able to see men and women, not just as they are, but as they might become. Whether it was the self-righteous Pharisee, an unscrupulous tax collector, or a fallen woman, he showed an interest in people, he stressed their future possibilities, and inspired them to achieve their best.

It is interesting to analyze the nature of Jesus' relationship to those he taught. It resembles what I have described in secular education as the "creative teacher-pupil relationship," a concept I developed in response to critics who asked me, "How can you teach children to think creatively? Don't you realize that the thinking processes are automatic, swift and spontaneous when they are not disturbed by other influences?" It was clear to me, however, that certain conditions in the teacher-pupil relationship and in the school situation interfere with this natural process. (The concept of the "creative teacher-pupil relationship" is described in the first chapter in this volume.)

As I read accounts of Jesus' relationship to his followers, I see an excellent example of the creative teacher-pupil relationship. He treated their questions and ideas with respect. He tried to understand what they were thinking, to push them on to think more deeply, more honestly, more searchingly, more penetratingly. He understood so well the obstacles to their thinking and living creatively. After all, to live creatively is to live truthfully.

PART II. EXPLORATORY STUDIES

SEX ROLES AND APPROPRIATENESS OF STIMULI IN TESTS OF CREATIVE THINKING

Some of the most firmly established facts now available about individual differences concern the rarity of women among inventors (Rossman, 1931) and creative scientists (Roe, 1956). Many have hastened to point out the apparent paradox between these and other equally well-established facts about the superior scholastic achievement, reading skills, and vocabulary development of girls (Mussen and Conger, 1956).

Both biological and social explanations have been offered for these phenomena (Bosselman, 1953). The biologist explains that the boy, by virtue of his usually stronger muscular endowment and his more active sexual role, is predisposed to more aggressive qualities. The girl, more receptive in her sexual and childbearing functions and less muscular, is predisposed to passivity. The sociologist points out that from the earliest months of life the child is confronted with expectations that he become a typical boy, she a typical girl. The boy is given toy guns, airplanes, and fire trucks. The girl is given a doll, a tea set, and a nurse's kit.

Psychologists have urged that boys and girls be given different sets of reading material in the early school years. Lecky (1945), for example, attributes the deficiency of boys in reading, as compared with girls who receive the same instruction, to a lack of reading material appropriate for boys from six to eight, rather than to a lack of ability. He points out that the boy from six to eight considers it extremely important to maintain the conception of himself as manly. He must not cry even if "it hurts," and likes to play cowboy, space-man, G-man, and the like. Lecky pictures the position of this same boy who must stand before his companions and read "the little red hen says, 'Cluck! Cluck! Cluck!'— or something equally inconsistent with his standards of how a boy should behave. Lecky contends that the boy's refusal to learn to read is in defense of his masculine values and as such is a wholesome, normal, and desirable kind of behavior. The damage resulting from his failure to

NOTE: The author is indebted to John E. Bowers for his assistance in preparing this chapter.

103

learn to read is, of course, obvious. It must be admitted, however, that many improvements have been made in elementary school reading materials since Lecky wrote in 1945.

In our experiment, an attempt was made to explore the problem of providing sex-appropriate materials for eliciting creative productivity among children in the early school years. It was expected that girls would produce a larger number of creative responses than boys to stimuli appropriate to the feminine role, but that boys would produce a larger number of such responses than girls to stimuli appropriate to masculine roles.

PROCEDURES

Subjects. The subjects of this experiment were 94 first graders, 79 second graders, and 86 third graders, the total enrollment of these grades in two elementary schools.

Testing Materials and Procedures. The testing materials, testing procedures, and scoring procedures have been described in a separate publication (Torrance, 1962). The task required the subjects to invent ways of improving toys "to make them more fun to play with." The typically feminine toy was a nurse's kit, available in almost any dime store or toy department. The typically masculine toy was a fire truck. In addition, a toy dog was used in an attempt to find a stimulus unrelated to sex role.

Inventing improvements for these two toys constituted three of the five items administered the subjects. The administration, through individual interviews, was accomplished by the author and research assistants and fellows of the Bureau of Educational Research at the University of Minnesota. The toys, one at a time in the order named, were placed in front of the subject where they could be handled and manipulated if the subject so desired. No time limit was imposed.

Data Analysis. All test records were scored by the senior author following a guide set up at the beginning of the project (Torrance, 1962). In brief, the fluency score, which is of major concern in this study, is simply the sum of the acceptable responses given for improving the toy. The flexibility score is the number of different approaches or principles used in improving the toy. These principles include magnification, minification, changing shape, changing color, giving sensory appeal (light, motion, odor), changing material, rearranging, changing position, improving quality, addition, subtraction, substitution, multiplication, division, and adapting to new use.

Means were computed for fluency and flexibility for males and females (separately within grades one, two, and three). Fluency and flexibility measures were obtained from responses to the nurse's kit, the fire truck, and the toy dog. Two hypotheses were tested in each grade on both fluency and flexibility scores:

1. Simultaneously, the mean for males equals the mean for females on the nurse's kit and the mean for males equals the mean for females on the fire truck.

$$M \text{ (male)} = M \text{ (female) on kit}$$
$$M \text{ (male)} = M \text{ (female) on truck}$$

2. The mean for males on the nurse's kit minus the mean for males on the fire truck equals the mean for females on the nurse's kit minus the mean for females on the fire truck.

$$M \text{ (male:kit)} - M \text{ (male:truck)} - M \text{ (female:truck)}$$

The computational technique for testing the first hypothesis, discussed by Heck (1958), involves post-multiplying the matrix of the between-sexes sums of squares and cross-products (H) by the inverse of the matrix of the within-sexes sums of squares and cross-products (E), and obtaining the matrix HE^{-1}. The characteristic roots of the matrix HE^{-1} are found and the following value (where λ max is the largest characteristic root) is calculated:

$$\frac{\lambda \max}{1 + \lambda \max}$$

If either the number of the groups is two ($k = 2$), or the number of variates is one ($p = 1$), the above value is distributed as the incomplete beta function with m' and n' degrees of freedom, where

$$m' = \frac{(k - p - 1) - 1}{2} + 1 \text{ and } n' = \frac{N - k - p - 1}{2} + 1,$$

$N =$ the total number of males and females in the calculation of n'.

The second hypothesis was tested by calculating the difference between each child's score on the fire-truck item and his score on the nurse-kit item. In each grade, a t-test between the sexes was calculated for these differences.

RESULTS

Mean fluency and flexibility scores in response to the three toys are presented in Table 4, for boys and girls in each of the first three grades. The trends represented by these data are delineated in Figure 11. In the first grade the girls tended to score higher on the kit than the boys, the boys scoring higher than the girls on the fire truck. Means for the

Table 4. Mean Fluency and Flexibility Scores in Response to Three Toys for Boys and Girls in the First Three Grades

Ability and Grade	Number		Kit		Truck		Dog	
	Boys	Girls	Boys	Girls	Boys	Girls	Boys	Girls
Fluency								
First	43	51	3.49	4.35	4.49	3.78	5.02	5.37
Second	35	44	5.60	6.07	8.51	6.66	8.03	7.43
Third	36	50	6.58	5.94	10.22	7.46	9.11	7.92
Flexibility								
First	43	51	1.70	1.88	2.70	2.37	2.84	3.16
Second	35	44	2.71	2.75	3.97	3.48	4.31	4.11
Third	36	50	3.08	2.82	5.03	4.10	4.86	4.64

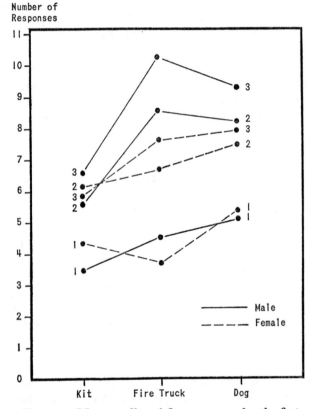

Figure 11. Mean profiles of fluency scores for the first three grades, by sex.

toy dog are almost identical, although the girls maintained a slight margin.

Ten of the forty-three first grade boys refused to make any response to the kit, while only two failed to make at least one suggestion for improving the fire truck. In addition, a number of the boys handled the kit situation psychologically by changing the nurse's kit to a doctor's kit before inventing improvements. A number of the boys, when confronted with the nurse's kit, would say in a weak, hurt manner, "But I'm not a girl." Only when assured that this was acknowledged and that "it was all right" were some of them willing to give any responses. No such protests were made by girls. Exactly the same number of girls (6 out of 51) failed the kit as failed the fire truck.

For the second grade, the difference in mean scores of boys and girls becomes narrower for the kit, wider for the fire truck, and reverses for the dog. For the third grade, the trend observed in the second grade becomes more pronounced, with boys tending to score higher than girls on all three toys.

In testing the first hypothesis, the data are of the following type: There are two variates (kit and truck) and responses to these two variates by two groups (boys and girls). Using the procedure developed by Heck (1958), we can test simultaneously the hypothesis that the boys' mean on the kit equals the girls' mean on the kit and that the boys' mean on the truck equals the girls' mean on the truck. If this hypothesis is rejected, we can test for similarity of profiles.

To accomplish this, we let H denote the matrix of between-groups sums of squares and cross-products and E denote the matrix of the within-groups sums of squares and cross-products of the two variates. Letting E^{-1} be the inverse of E, HE^{-1} was calculated. Letting λ_1 be the largest characteristic root of HE^{-1}, the following value was calculated:

$$\frac{\lambda 1}{1 + \lambda 1}$$

If this value is greater than $x\gamma$, the hypothesis can be rejected; if less than $x\alpha$, the hypothesis can be accepted. The value $x\gamma$ is obtained from Incomplete Beta Function Tables with

$$\frac{(1, N - 3)}{2}$$

degrees of freedom, where $N = N_1 + N_2$. Applying this procedure to the fluency scores, the hypothesis was accepted for the first grade and rejected for the second and third grades at the .05 level. When the procedure is applied to flexibility scores, the hypothesis is accepted for all three grades.

By following the procedure already outlined for testing the second hypothesis, the results shown in Table 5 were obtained. It will be observed that these results are essentially the same as those obtained above. If we are willing to accept the .07 level of significance, however, the difference for the first grade on fluency may be regarded as significant.

Table 5. Mean Differences of Fluency and Flexibility Scores (Fire Truck Minus Nurse's Kit) and Tests of Significance of Differences between Boys and Girls

Ability and Grade	Boys M.D.	Girls (FT−NK)	t-ratio	Degree of Freedom	P
Fluency					
First	1.000	−0.569	1.87	92	<.07
Second	2.914	0.591	2.60	77	<.05
Third	3.639	1.520	2.77	84	<.01
Flexibility					
First	1.000	0.490	1.44	92	.20−.10
Second	1.257	0.727	1.14	77	<.20
Third	1.944	1.280	1.59	84	.20−.10

DISCUSSION AND CONCLUSIONS

Only in the first grade do we find much evidence to support the contention that boys and girls should be provided materials appropriate to sex role in order to elicit creative or inventive ideas. Several factors should be considered, however, in interpreting these findings. First, it must be recognized that the tests were conducted in the presence of a single, accepting adult and not in the presence of peers. Consequently, resistance to responding to a stimulus inappropriate to sex role may have been reduced. Furthermore, many of the boys had to be reassured before they would respond to the nurse's kit, which some converted into a masculine toy by treating it as a doctor's kit.

Perhaps the most surprising finding of the study is the increasing superiority of boys over girls on this type of thinking, beginning with the second grade. It will be recalled that by the third grade, boys tended to produce more inventive ideas than girls for all three toys.

Apparently, whatever factors explain the rarity of women among inventors and creative scientists may begin operating as early as the second or third grade. In interpreting these findings, it must be remembered that the task used requires the subject to be sensitive to defects and to invent improvements. It may be that lessons stressing the importance of accepting the status quo are being learned more thoroughly by girls than by boys during the early school years. If the creative talents of women are to be used in science and technology, perhaps efforts in this direction should not be delayed until the college years.

SUMMARY

This experiment was designed to study the importance of providing stimuli appropriate to sex role in eliciting creative or inventive ideas among children in the early school years. The subjects were 259 children in the first, second, and third grades of two elementary schools. Each subject was administered individually and orally a test that required him to invent ideas for improving a nurse's kit, a fire truck, and a toy dog, so that they "would be more fun to play with." The nurse's kit was selected as a typically feminine toy; the fire truck, as a typically masculine toy, and the toy dog, as appropriate for both boys and girls.

Fluency and flexibility scores were obtained for each subject on each toy. First grade boys compared with first grade girls tended to produce fewer responses to the nurse's kit and more responses to the fire truck. Observations made by experimenters provided further evidence on the reluctance of boys to respond to the nurse's kit. In the second grade, the superiority of the girls on the nurse's kit diminished and the superiority of the boys on the fire truck increased. By the third grade, boys tended to be superior to girls on all three toys. When the mean profiles of girls and boys were compared, differences in the first grade were found to be significant at about the .07 level. In the second grade, differences in mean profiles were significant at better than the .05 level and in the third grade at better than the .01 per cent level.

The findings suggest that it is desirable to provide stimuli appropriate to sex roles (1) for the purpose of eliciting creative thinking at the first-grade level and (2) for developing more effective techniques of encouraging girls in the second and third grades to cultivate their inventiveness.

THE ROLE OF MANIPULATION IN
CREATIVE THINKING

EARLY in the process of administering our test of creative thinking to children in the first and second grades, members of the project staff observed what appeared to be a meaningful relationship between the child's manipulation of the objects provided to evoke creative thinking, or inventiveness, and the quantity and quality of his responses. Since we were unable to find any information of a firm nature concerning the role of manipulation in creative thinking and inventiveness, the present study was undertaken to investigate the relationship between degree of manipulation and the quantity and quality of responses.

Rossman (1931), in his study of the psychology of inventors, assigns an important role to manipulative tendencies in inventiveness, but offers little or no scientific data in support of his contention. He maintains that an irresistible tendency to manipulate and explore objects begins at an early stage and is probably the basis of curiosity and playfulness. In his opinion, manipulation supplies much of the necessary experience for the development of imagination.

Indirect support for this idea may be inferred from recent research findings that differentiate highly creative individuals from less creative ones. Barron (1958), for example, says that his more original subjects showed a marked preference for complex, asymmetrical, and vital or dynamic drawings and paintings. Theoretically, such subjects might be expected to be more willing to manipulate objects and to risk the possibility of upsetting the existing balance. Stein's less creative research chemists were more inclined than the highly creative ones to try for a quick solution by chance; the latter preferred to allow hypotheses for solution to be developed from within the problem rather than attempt to superimpose hypotheses prematurely from without (Quillian, 1957).

The present study hypothesized, first, that the degree of manipulation of objects designed to evoke creative thinking is related to the quantity

NOTE: The author is indebted to Frank B. Baker and John E. Bowers for their assistance in preparing this chapter.

110

and quality of responses given; and second, that boys tend to manipulate such objects more than do girls.

Subjects. The subjects were first, second, and third graders enrolled in two elementary schools. Systematic recording of observations concerning manipulation was not begun until the test had been administered to one first and one second grade class. Data were obtained for 68 first graders, 62 second graders, and 82 third graders.

Data Collection. The data were collected during the individual administration of a test of creative thinking to the subjects. The test materials, administration procedures, and scoring system have been described in detail elsewhere (Torrance, 1962). In brief, the task required the subjects to invent ways of improving a nurse's kit, a fire truck, and a toy dog, so that "they would be more fun to play with"; to list the possible courses of action that Mother Hubbard could have taken on finding no food in her cupboard; and to list the possible consequences of the cow's jumping over the moon. Responses evoked by the toy-problems were scored for fluency (number of improvements suggested) and flexibility (number of different approaches used in making the improvements). Responses to the other two problems, of only secondary interest in this study, were scored for fluency and for originality (all responses other than those commonly associated with the nursery rhymes and other than the most obvious ones).

In classifying the degree of manipulation, three categories were used. In the "low" category were placed those who did not handle the toys at all; in the "medium," those who manipulated one or more toys but not to a high degree; and in the "high," those whose manipulation was labeled by the examiner as "considerable," "extreme," "excessive," "high degree," and the like.

Analysis of Data. In order to test the effects of degree of manipulation on performance of the test tasks, the data were subjected to analysis of variance. The data for each grade were treated separately and within each grade; fluency and flexibility scores on the toys and fluency and originality scores on the Mother-Hubbard and Cow-Jumping problems were each analyzed separately. After performing the usual analyses of variance, the high- and medium-manipulation groups were combined and compared with the low-manipulation (actually no manipulation) group according to a technique described by Scheffe (1953).

In order to study the independence of sex and manipulative tendency, by grade level, chi-square analyses were performed.

RESULTS

Mean fluency and flexibility scores in response to the toy-improvement problems for the high-, medium-, and low-manipulation groups within each grade are shown in Table 6. Each grade level shows a consistent tendency for mean scores to be related to degree of manipulation. These trends are presented graphically in Figure 12.

Similar data are presented in Table 7 and Figure 13 for scores on the Mother-Hubbard and Cow-Jumping problems, neither one permitting manipulation of objects. Although many of the differences in means are minute, the same trends observed in the toy-problem data persist.

To test the significance of the observed trends, analyses of variance were performed to determine the effects of degree of manipulation on scores. Data testing the effects of degree of manipulation on fluency scores on the toy-improvement problems are presented in Table 8. The degree of manipulation has a significant effect on fluency scores at all three grade levels. When nonmanipulators are compared with ma-

Table 6. Mean Scores on Toy-Improvement Problems by High-, Medium-, and Low-Manipulation Groups in the First Three Grades

Ability and Grade	Number	Mean Score		
		High	Medium	Low
Fluency				
First	68	17.44	15.12	7.62
Second	62	31.94	20.97	11.69
Third	82	29.50	24.32	13.45
Flexibility				
First	68	8.33	7.70	4.65
Second	62	14.18	11.25	6.15
Third	82	14.25	12.91	8.32

Table 7. Mean Scores on Mother-Hubbard and Cow-Jumping Problems by High-, Medium-, and Low-Manipulation Groups in the First Three Grades

Ability and Grade	Number	Mean Score		
		High	Medium	Low
Fluency				
First	68	9.22	6.66	4.31
Second	62	13.18	8.03	7.38
Third	82	11.62	11.27	7.27
Originality				
First	68	2.89	2.58	1.54
Second	62	8.06	4.59	3.62
Third	82	8.19	6.82	4.27

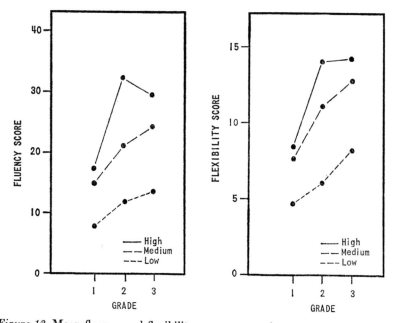

Figure 12. Mean fluency and flexibility scores on toy-improvement problems of high-, medium-, and low-manipulation groups in grades one, two, and three.

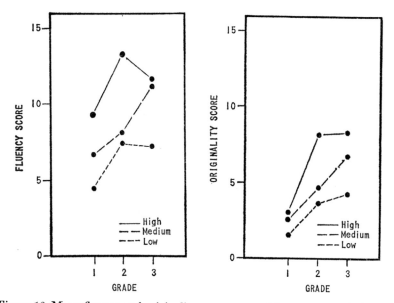

Figure 13. Mean fluency and originality scores on problems not permitting manipulation, of high-, medium-, and low-manipulation groups in grades one, two, and three.

113

Table 8. Analysis of Variance Data to Test Significance of Effects of Degree of
Manipulation on Fluency Scores for Toy-Improvement Problems
in the First Three Grades

Source of Variance	Sum of Squares	Degree of Freedom	Mean Squares	F-ratio	P	Scheffe's Test
First grade						
Between-group (high, med., low)	1,066.87	2		5.62	<.01	<.05
Within-group	6,173.89	65	94.98			
Total	7,240.76	67				
Second grade						
Between-group (high, med., low)	3,095.26	2		7.21	<.01	<.01
Within-group	12,670.68	59	214.76			
Total	15,765.94	61				
Third grade						
Between-group (high, med., low)	2,728.90	2		6.74	<.01	<.01
Within-group	15,989.00	79	202.39			
Total	18,717.90	81				

Table 9. Analysis of Variance Data to Test Significance of Effects of Degree of
Manipulation on Flexibility Scores for Toy-Improvement Problems in the
First Three Grades

Source of Variance	Sum of Squares	Degree of Freedom	Mean Squares	F-ratio	P	Scheffe's Test
First grade						
Between-group (high, med., low)	165.20	2		6.57	<.01	<.01
Within-group	816.85	65	12.57			
Total	982.05	67				
Second grade						
Between-group (high, med., low)	478.82	2		9.00	<.01	<.01
Within-group	1,570.16	59	26.61			
Total	2,048.98	61				
Third grade						
Between-group (high, med., low)	415.29	2		8.39	<.01	<.01
Within-group	1,955.41	79	24.75			
Total	2,370.70	81				

nipulators on the basis of Scheffe's test, the effects are significant at all three grade levels.

Similar data concerning flexibility scores are presented in Table 9. Again, the effects are significant at all three levels. The higher the degree of manipulation, the higher the mean scores in each manipulation category.

Data to test the effects of degree of manipulation on fluency and originality scores on the Mother-Hubbard and Cow-Jumping problems are presented in Tables 10 and 11. Except for the fluency scores of the first grade, the effects of degree of manipulation are not statistically significant.

The number of boys and girls engaging in each degree of manipulation at each grade level and their chi-square results are shown in Table 12. Differences in the first grade are not statistically significant. By the second grade, manipulative tendencies are greater among boys than among girls. By the third grade, these differences have become quite marked.

In Table 13 the data presented in Table 12 have been rearranged to show differences from grade to grade among boys and among girls separately. The tendency for boys to become more manipulative increases steadily and significantly from grade to grade, from the first through the third. No such tendency exists among girls, however.

Table 10. Analysis of Variance Data to Test Significance of Effects of Degree of Manipulation on Fluency Scores on Mother-Hubbard and Cow-Jumping Problems in the First Three Grades

Source of Variance	Sum of Squares	Degree of Freedom	Mean Squares	F-ratio	P	Scheffe's Test
First grade						
Between-group (high, med., low)	181.85	2		3.30	$<.05$	$<.05$
Within-group 1,792.43	1,792.43	65	27.58			
Total 1,974.28	1,974.28	67				
Second grade						
Between-group (high, med., low)	354.66	2		2.84	n.s.	n.s.
Within-group 3,678.52	3,678.52	59	62.35			
Total 4,033.18	4,033.18	61				
Third grade						
Between-group (high, med., low)	271.26	2		1.72	n.s.	n.s.
Within-group 6,246.84	6,246.84	79	79.07			
Total 6,518.10	6,518.10	81				

Table 11. Analysis of Variance Data to Test Significance of Effects of Degree of Manipulation on Originality Scores on Mother-Hubbard and Cow-Jumping Problems in the First Three Grades

Source of Variance	Sum of Squares	Degree of Freedom	Mean Squares	F-ratio	P	Scheffe's Test
First grade						
Between-group (high, med., low)	20.28	2		1.76	n.s.	n.s.
Within-group	375.41	65	5.78			
Total	395.69	67				
Second grade						
Between-group (high, med., low)	182.15	2		2.15	n.s.	n.s.
Within-group	2,495.74	59	42.30			
Total	2,677.89	61				
Third grade						
Between-group (high, med., low)	158.37	2		1.83	n.s.	n.s.
Within-group	3,421.35	79	43.31			
Total	3,579.72	81				

If we break down each set of chi-squares, the following patterns appear: (1) In the chi-squares in Table 13, the pattern for girls is the same from grade to grade but boys differ in manipulative tendencies from grade to grade. (2) In those in Table 12, boys and girls are alike with respect to manipulative tendencies in grade one, are significantly different in grade two, and are a great deal different in grade three.

The male pattern in grade one and the female pattern in all three grades are alike, the male pattern in grade two is not like the female pattern, and in grade three the male pattern is even more dissimilar.

Table 12. Number of Boys and Girls Engaging in Varying Degrees of Manipulation in the First Three Grades

Degree	First Grade			Second Grade			Third Grade		
	Boys	Girls	Total	Boys	Girls	Total	Boys	Girls	Total
High	5	4	9	11	6	17	11	5	16
Medium	16	17	33	16	16	32	24	20	44
Low	12	14	26	2	11	13	1	21	22
Total	33	35	68	29	33	62	36	46	82

NOTE: χ^2 (first grade) $= 0.2365$; $df = 2$; n.s.
χ^2 (second grade) $= 7.4742$; $df = 2$; $P < .02$
χ^2 (third grade) $= 19.8715$; $df = 2$; $P < .001$
χ^2 (over-all) $= 27.5822$; $df = 6$; $P < .001$

Table 13. Number of First, Second, and Third Graders Engaging in Varying Degrees of
Manipulation for Boys and Girls

| | Boys | | | | Girls | | | |
Degree	First Grade	Second Grade	Third Grade	Total	First Grade	Second Grade	Third Grade	Total
High	5	11	11	27	4	6	5	15
Medium	16	16	24	56	17	16	20	53
Low	12	2	1	15	14	11	21	46
Total	33	29	36	98	35	33	46	114

NOTE: χ^2 (boys) = 18.7208; $df = 4$; $P < .001$
χ^2 (girls) = 1.7698; $df = 4$; n.s.
χ^2 (over-all) = 20.4906; $df = 8$; $P < .01$

DISCUSSION AND CONCLUSIONS

From the data, it seems clear that in the tasks permitting manipulation of objects, degree of manipulation significantly affects the number and flexibility of responses. This effect, however, does not appear to generalize significantly to problems not permitting manipulation of objects. These results suggest that when we attempt to evoke inventive responses, subjects should be encouraged to manipulate the objects involved. They also suggest the need for devising means whereby children can imaginatively manipulate ideas and relationships where manual manipulation is not possible. Experiments involving pictures, making drawings, role-playing, and the like are needed to test the effects of the manipulation of ideas possible through such techniques.

Even though boys tend to engage in more manipulation of objects than girls, this tendency does not become significant until about the second grade. These results should be viewed in relation to the findings above and to those of the study preceding this one, showing that in the first three grades boys tend to become increasingly more inventive than girls. Although it cannot be concluded with firmness that permitting and encouraging girls to engage in a greater degree of manipulation will increase their productivity and flexibility in creative activities, the recommendation seems worthy of consideration.

The findings of this study support the contention of Rossman (1931) that the manipulative tendencies are important in the psychology of invention. They suggest the need for reviewing and re-evaluating earlier theories about the development of manipulative tendencies in children. To encourage inventiveness, it would seem desirable to stimulate and implement, and thus keep alive, the natural inclination to manipulate and experiment with objects and ideas.

SUMMARY

One objective of this study was to explore the effects of manipulation on the quantity and quality of ideas produced in response to problems permitting and to problems not permitting manipulation of objects. A second objective was to determine what differences in manipulativeness exist between boys and girls and among grades.

In the administration of a test of creative thinking, records of manipulative activities were compiled for 68 first graders, 62 second graders, and 82 third graders. Tasks permitting manipulation of objects required subjects to invent improvements for a nurse's kit, a fire truck, and a toy dog. Tasks not permitting manual manipulation required them to elaborate the stories of Mother Hubbard and the Cow Who Jumped over the Moon. Fluency and flexibility scores on the toy-improvement problems and fluency and originality scores on the other problems were obtained for each subject. Three degrees of manipulation were used: high, medium (any observable degree), and low (no manipulation).

In tasks permitting manipulation of objects (toy-improvement), it was found that degree of manipulation significantly affected both fluency and flexibility. This effect, however, did not seem to transfer to problems not permitting manipulation of objects (Mother Hubbard and Cow). It was also found that boys engage in more manipulation of objects than girls but that this tendency does not become significant until the second grade. From grade to grade, the tendency of boys to manipulate increases whereas that of girls shows no significant change. These results support theories projected in earlier research on the importance of manipulativeness in creative and inventive activities.

PEER SANCTIONS AGAINST HIGHLY
CREATIVE CHILDREN

CREATIVE persons have always met with opposition. Columbus was scorned for thinking the world was round. Everyone laughed at the Wright brothers for believing men could fly. It seems to be the lot of innovators in all fields to endure opposition, apathy, prejudice, and even hate. Only strong confidence in their beliefs enabled the great thinkers of history to persevere in the face of opposition. This pattern of self-confidence versus opposition has become so much a part of our culture that many people regard it as a necessary prerequisite to outstanding success as a creative scientist or inventive genius. Whether or not this state of affairs must be accepted as a permanent part of our culture, children should certainly develop at an early age a feeling of confidence in their own original ideas and perceptions. Parents and teachers can do much to encourage this attitude.

Psychologists and sociologists have long recognized in industry the process of "rate setting" and the negative sanctions brought against the "rate buster" by the work group. Educators likewise have been aware of the sanctions against the high achiever or "curve buster." Any degree of outstanding success seems to cut off the unique member from his group and the pressure generated against uniqueness tends to militate against high achievement. The sanctions against the most creative member of a group are of a slightly different order. His ideas are "new, unusual, unorthodox, a step into the unknown." Not knowing how to evaluate them, the group is puzzled about how to treat them. Other members tend to ignore, oppose, or ridicule his ideas — apparently the only technique they have for coping with them. Obviously, the group is capable of placing the highly creative person in an uncomfortable situation.

For this study, a situation was set up in which the strategies of groups in coping with the contributions of highly creative members and the counterstrategies of the most creative member could be observed. The study is admittedly exploratory, and even the taxonomy of strategies

119

identified needs to be extended by similar studies of other types of groups.

PROCEDURES

Subjects. The subjects of the study were 125 elementary school pupils, 25 at each grade level from the second through the sixth grades. Each class of 25 pupils was divided into five five-person groups. Groups were formed by ranking all pupils in each class on the basis of scores on a test of creative thinking administered in a previous study and placing in each group one of the five most creative, one of the next five, and so on. The scheme below shows how the groups were formed according to rank on the test of creativity:

Group 1: 1, 6, 11, 16, 21
Group 2: 2, 7, 12, 17, 22
Group 3: 3, 8, 13, 18, 23
Group 4: 4, 9, 14, 19, 24
Group 5: 5, 10, 15, 20, 25

The object of the group composition was to maximize and make as constant as possible the distance between the most creative member and the remainder of the group on the creativity variable. In each group there were either two boys and three girls or two girls and three boys. In a few groups one member was absent at the time of the experiment, but no group consisted of less than four members.

Experimental Procedure. In each class all five groups were tested simultaneously, each in a different room. In an attempt to maximize the group's willingness to utilize its talent, prizes of interesting science books were offered for the best *group* or *team* performance. In the orientation, the terms "group" and "team" were emphasized. To simplify the recording of observations and the reporting of results, each subject was given a colored arm band according to his rank in the five-person group on the creativity test, as follows: First: White; Second: Gold; Third: Red; Fourth: Green; Fifth: Blue. The subjects were, of course, not informed concerning the significance of the different colors.

Each group was provided a box of science toys and toy parts (Science Toy Collection No. 2, The Library of Science, 59 Fourth Avenue, New York 3, N.Y.), which included a sparkler, a finger trap, a pin trick, a four-ball puzzle, a topsy turvy top, a broken jumping top, a blow ball, parts of a broken flying saucer, nutty putty, a magnifying glass, a compass, a whistle, and a magnet. Each group was given twenty-five minutes in which to explore and experiment to discover what could be done with the toys and toy parts and why they function as they do. Then five minutes was allowed in which to plan a demonstration. Following this, the group demonstrated and explained the principles that could be taught with the toys and toy parts. The time limit for the demonstration was twenty-five minutes. Finally, each subject was asked to rank each member of the group according to the value of his contribution to the group's success. This was done by having each member arrange in order five slips of colored paper corresponding to the colors of the arm bands.

The experimenters tabulated the number of ideas initiated by each subject during the exploratory phase and recorded all ideas demonstrated and explained during the demonstration period. Experimenters also described how the group organized itself and got underway with the task, what kind of roles developed for White (the most creative), how the group went about planning the demonstration, what role or roles White played in planning, what role White was assigned in the demonstration, and other behaviors of the group — particularly actions directed toward White.

In determining winners, one point was awarded for each idea demonstrated and for each correct explanation.

RESULTS

Two kinds of results are reported: (a) summary statistics for all the groups and (b) descriptive data on the behavior of each group.

Summary Findings. In spite of the social pressures against the most creative member, evident in practically every group, 17 of the 25 (68 per cent) succeeded in initiating the largest number of ideas in their respective groups during the exploratory phase. In several other cases, the most creative member initiated only one idea less than the top contributor in this respect. This provides a rough validation of the measure of creativity used. Only 6 of the 25 (24 per cent), however, were rated by the group as making the most valuable contribution to the group's success.

To determine the degree of agreement within groups concerning the value of contributions to the group's success the Kendall Coefficient of Concordance (Kendall, 1948) was computed for each group. (This was not possible for one of the sixth-grade groups because the experimenter did not have the subjects include themselves in the rankings.) There was a general trend for the degree of agreement to increase gradually from the second through the sixth grade. In the sixth grade the hypothesis of no relation among the rankings was rejected for three of the four groups at less than the .01 level of significance and in the remaining group, at about the .05 level. In the second grade only one group showed significance at the .05 level; the others showed nonsignificant relations among rankings.

For many groups it was observed that the girls engaged in little manipulation and assumed feminine airs of helplessness in explaining why the toys worked as they did. In order to determine whether this observation could be supported statistically, boys and girls at each grade level were compared on number of ideas initiated, number of ideas presented, and number of ideas explained. The means and tests of significance are shown in Table 14.

Table 14. Means and Tests of Significance of Differences in Means for Boys and Girls on Number of Ideas Initiated, Number of Ideas Demonstrated, and Number of Ideas Explained

Grade	Mean (Init.)			Mean (Demon.)			Mean (Expl.)		
	Boys	Girls	F-ratio	Boys	Girls	F-ratio	Boys	Girls	F-ratio
Second	5.2	3.7	1.37	3.6	2.0	3.62†	1.9	0.9	4.68*
Third	8.1	5.5	2.54	4.4	3.2	1.02	3.1	2.0	1.44
Fourth	7.3	4.5	4.08†	5.6	2.2	9.76*	4.0	0.8	8.90*
Fifth	7.0	8.7	0.46	6.7	3.1	3.48	4.6	1.3	3.05†
Sixth	8.8	7.9	0.10	5.9	3.0	6.21*	7.1	3.5	4.09†
All grades pooled	7.4	5.9	2.46	5.5	2.7	21.58*	4.0	1.6	18.05*

* Significant at .05 level or better.

† Significant at .10 level or better.

Except at the fifth-grade level, the boys tended to initiate more ideas than the girls during the exploratory period. The observed difference, however, is statistically significant at only the fourth-grade level. The reversal of this trend in the fifth grade is apparently a part of a general tendency for girls to show a spurt in development of creative thinking abilities during the fifth grade. Many of the contributions credited to the girls, however, were of a nature that might be called "idle talk" rather than coming to grips with the task. Many of them made clear their feeling that girls were not expected "to know about this kind of thing." Some made little or no attempt even to manipulate the toys.

The data for number of ideas demonstrated and number of ideas explained are more conclusive. The trend in both cases is consistent at all grade levels; over-all, the boys demonstrated and explained twice as many ideas as the girls. The differences in mean number of ideas demonstrated are statistically significant for the second, fourth, and sixth grades. The mean number of ideas explained shows statistically significant differences at all grade levels except the third.

GROUP BEHAVIOR

Second-Grade Groups. In the first group White was absent, so Gold may be regarded as the most creative member of this group. The subjects immediately grabbed the toys and began to explain them to each other. Gold collected most of the items and said, "I'll show and tell these. I know all about these." Green competed to get some of the items away from her. At one point Gold said, "Only the boys can get the rocket to work." Green made an attempt to introduce goal-orientation, saying "We gotta be serious now. We gotta talk." These attempts had little effect, however, and the group continued in a disorganized manner. Having initiated 22 ideas during the exploratory period, the group demonstrated 12 and explained 5 during the final period. All agreed that Green made the most valuable contribution to the group's success. Degree of agreement on the value of the different contributions is significant (Kendall's $\omega = .625$) at about the .05 level. Rankings from most to least valuable were: Green, Gold, Red, and Blue.

Members of the second group eagerly grabbed the toys and started to question the experimenter about them. White was quiet and worked alone, seemingly interested in the toys but offering no comment. Later she did offer a few ideas but received no response from the other members. No organization emerged except that it was agreed they would just "go around the table" in giving their demonstrations. There was considerable scrambling for possession of the toys, each wanting a toy another had. Throughout the exploratory period the subjects tended to play individually, without listening to one another. White was not at all hopeful concerning the success of the group and predicted that Group 4 would win because "they have all of the good ones." The group initiated 17 ideas, demonstrated 9, and explained 5. There was little agreement about who made the most valuable contribution to the group's success (Kendall's $\omega = .35$, not significant). Over-all rankings from most to least valuable were as follows: Blue, Green, Gold, Red, and White.

Each member of the third group grabbed a toy and as soon as it was dropped someone else picked it up. There was considerable bickering throughout the procedure and eventually each had a pile of toys in front of him. White and Green squabbled over the possession of toys. Very few ideas were initiated as most of the energy was expended in bickering. White engaged almost entirely in individual activity, making comments now and then. These comments made no impact whatsoever upon the group. The only organized action was the determination of sequence in the demonstration. No identification with the group, nor any cooperative behavior among members, was evident. There was almost no agreement about who made the most valuable contribution to the group's success (Kendall's $\omega = .20$). Rankings were as follows: Red, Green, Gold, Blue, and White. The group initiated 12 ideas, demonstrated 12, and explained 5.

In Group 4 the members worked independently and in general ignored one another. White was domineering toward Red but otherwise everyone ignored the comments of the others. White was inquisitive and enthusiastic, running all over the place, trying things out, and quarrelling with Red. The group developed no cohesiveness and made no effort to organize. White was particularly active and initiated about half the ideas suggested during the exploratory period but he showed no responsibility toward the group, laughing, shouting, and acting like a "spoiled child." In spite of his high productivity during the exploratory period, he demonstrated and explained only one idea. At one point when another member presented an idea initiated by White in the exploratory period, White screamed, "You're stealing my brains. It's not nice to steal other people's brains!" The group initiated 36 ideas, demonstrated 8, and explained 4, the poorest performance of the five second-grade groups. There was little agreement on the relative value of contributions (Kendall's $\omega = .19$). White, Red, and Green tied for highest rank, with Blue and Gold following.

As in the other groups, the members of Group 5 plunged into the box of toys eagerly. The two girls, White and Red, sat together at the table and played with the toys they could obtain. White was quite aggressive and initiated more ideas than anyone else, but Red was extremely quiet. The boys were extremely active, running about the room, testing out the toys, fighting over possession of them. White expressed enjoyment of the process at the beginning but soon lost interest and insisted that the experimenter let them do something else, saying, "I'm sick of this!" repeatedly and ill-naturedly. She insisted that "ladies be first" in the demonstration and distracted rather than supported the attempts of the others to demonstrate and explain ideas. Group goals had no meaning for this group; no cooperative behavior was shown, nor did the members even listen to one another's explanations. Green possessed an unusually large amount of scientific information, apparently taught him by his father. For example, he gave an excellent explanation of the principles of physics involved in the functioning of the magnifying glass. He came forth with his ideas only after everyone else had run out of ideas, or when the others demonstrated something and could not explain it. This group initiated 16 ideas, demonstrated 21, and explained 11, by far the best performance of the second-grade groups. With the exception of

White, the members recognized the value of Green's contribution. Moderate but not statistically significant agreement on rank (Kendall's $\omega =$ .42) produced the following order: Green, Gold, Red, White, and Blue.

In summary, the second-grade groups displayed a rather primitive level of group behavior. Little structure, little mutual support and cooperation emerged; the prevailing atmosphere was one of "survival of the fittest." Being a member of a group or team apparently meant nothing to these children. Although temporary coalitions of two members were formed in some groups, members most often worked independently and ignored everyone else. In general, the most creative children behaved like "spoiled brats," irresponsible insofar as the accomplishment of group goals was concerned. None of them was rated "most valuable" except for one three-way tie. Three, however, initiated the largest number of ideas in their groups. Furthermore, almost no agreement on the value of the contributions was reached.

Third-Grade Groups. Behavior of the first group was characterized by the "I know what this is!" response. No evidence of group organization or role differentiation was discerned. White, a relative newcomer to the class from Great Britain, initiated more ideas in the exploratory period than anyone else and absorbed much good-natured chiding from the remainder of the group. What little leadership emerged was exercised by Gold. There was a considerable amount of verbal kibitzing during the demonstrations, Green interrupting more than anyone else. A low level of agreement on who made the most valuable contribution to group success was reached, and only about one point separated the members in total rankings: White, Blue, Gold, Green. Red was absent. The group initiated 37 ideas, demonstrated 15, and explained 9, which placed the group third.

In the second group each member immediately grabbed a toy and proceeded to work individually. After about five minutes they entered into group activity, but not for long. All were seated around the table for only five minutes and then wandered off. No group effort was sustained for more than two or three minutes. White, a small, timid-appearing girl, did considerable individual work; others asked her questions, and near the end she offered some suggestions. In organizing for the demonstration, Green's suggestion to observe an alphabetical order was accepted. The entire group listened to White's demonstration and explanation. Although there was a low level of agreement on the relative value of member contributions, White was ranked highest. Gold and Green tied for second, followed by Red and Blue. The group initiated 26 ideas, demonstrated 10, and explained 8, tying for last place.

The third group developed no formal structure and made no attempt at even a minimal organization. White was passive and aloof, working alone. That no one paid her any attention seemed not to bother her. Gold, a boy, recognized as the scientist in the group, was enthusiastic throughout the procedure. Gold engaged in more manipulation of the toys than anyone else. During the exploratory period, White displayed her ingenuity, fastening nutty putty to a thread so she could bounce the putty around without losing it or having to run after it. Green then took little patches of nutty putty and fastened them to the side of the red top, making a human face, saying, "He has a big smile!" Significant agreement on the relative importance of the contributions produced the following order: Gold, Blue, Green, and White. The group initiated 38 ideas, demonstrated 10, and explained 8, tying with Group 2 for last place.

The group entered into the task enthusiastically. White vacillated between being quiet and being an authoritarian leader. He suggested that members raise their hands to talk, asked Blue and Gold not to "hog" the toys, and recommended following an alphabetical order in presenting their demonstrations. Throughout most of the exploratory period White worked alone, engaging in considerable manipulation of the toys, going out to fill the rocket with water, and similar activities. Gold was enthusiastic, captured attention often, and added to the demonstration after others had run out of ideas, reflecting considerable knowledge of scientific principles. Agreement concerning the relative value of contributions was statistically significant, resulting in the following order: Gold, Blue, Red, White, Green. The group initiated 31 ideas, demonstrated 30, and explained 20. This performance was the best in the class.

The fifth group plunged into the task enthusiastically, without organization, and with considerable quarrelling over possession of the toys. In general, the group was more interested in playing than in discovering and explaining principles. White monopolized the sparkler, becoming so preoccupied with it that he gave little attention to the other toys. Only once through trickery did another member manage to gain possession of the sparkler. Red assigned members an order of precedence for presenting the demonstrations but his efforts were ignored. White announced that he would demonstrate the sparkler and did an outstanding job of this narrow specialty, demonstrating and explaining five distinct scientific principles. All attempts to assume leadership were ignored. Blue, a girl, tried to introduce a goal-orientation but no one paid any attention to this effort. The group initiated 18 ideas, demonstrated 18, and explained 12, placing second in the standing. Agreement on the relative merit of contributions was statistically significant, the following order resulting: Red, Gold, Blue, and White. Actually, White gave the group more points than anyone else; the value of his contribution was probably not appreciated because of the narrowness of his interests, his aloofness, and his reluctance to share the sparkler with others.

In summary, then, the third-grade groups manifested scarcely less primitive behavior than the second-grade groups. There were more attempts at leadership, or attempts to obtain goal-orientation — toward winning the prize — but such attempts were generally ignored. The most creative members worked independently, unconcerned at being ignored for the most part. Other group members appeared to give more attention to the creative contributions, two of which were voted the "most valuable." All five of the most creative members ranked high in initiating ideas, three first and the other two, second.

Fourth-Grade Groups. In the first group, each member immediately grabbed a toy and began to manipulate it. Some yelled that they knew how this or that toy worked and there were many "what's that for's?" Throughout the procedure, members worked in pairs rather than as a group. White initiated the largest number of ideas, teaming with Gold. He made a number of suggestions to the other members and emerged as something of a leader near the end of the exploratory period. Gold tended to dominate in planning the demonstrations. White made his presentation first and more or less directed the order of the remaining demonstrations, contributing to the orderliness of the process. The group was active but quite disorganized. There was little agreement on ranking the contributions, although the following order was established: Gold, White, Red, Green, and Blue. The group initiated 28 ideas, demonstrated 14, and explained 8, tying with the fourth group for last place.

The second group was hesitant at first, but the boys soon began to advance ideas. Gold attempted to influence the group to consider one toy at a time and continued efforts to maintain goal-orientation with such requests as, "Let's start getting some scientific facts!" Red, a girl, said to Gold, "Say, Genius, how does this work?" Both Gold and the girls (Red and Green) on several occasions asked White's opinion, but White made no attempt to push himself forward. On one occasion, Gold asked White to find out about the magnet, write it out, and "put it in good English." White made no attempt to exercise leadership, responded when directed to write by Gold, but in general was content to manipulate the toys, make observations, and follow Gold's leadership. Agreement on the merit of contributions was high (significant at the .01 level), with the following rankings: Gold, White, Red, Green, and Blue. The group initiated 24 ideas, demonstrated 14, and explained 9, placing third in the standing.

The members of the third group each immediately reached for a toy, silently looked at it, and began to manipulate it. For the most part, members worked independently and silently. White wrote her ideas on paper, remarking three times, "I've got something on all except this and this . . ." On several occasions, two grabbed the same toy but one would relent, creating an atmosphere of cooperation. When the time for demonstration came, White announced, "I'm going to do these." During the exploratory period, her opinion was not sought by other members and no one paid much attention to her. Agreement on the merit of contributions was statistically significant ($<.01$), yielding the following order: Gold, Blue, Green, White, and Red. The group initiated 33 ideas, demonstrated 22, and explained 13, a performance that won the group second place.

The fourth group was from beginning to end casual and conversational. No formal structure of any kind developed. White was the last to demonstrate, had more toys than anyone else, initiated the largest number of ideas, and demonstrated what the others were unable to demonstrate and explain. Individual members never responded to the ideas of others, either ignoring them or accepting them as self-evident. Agreement on ranking contributions was not statistically significant, with the following order of merit: Gold, Green, White, Red, and Blue. The group initiated 32 ideas, demonstrated 16, and explained 6, tying with the first group for the lowest position.

Members of the fifth group started to experiment immediately. White was most industrious here, standing off by himself and working out his ideas alone. Gold also worked alone a few times but otherwise members worked in pairs, with the membership of pairs shifting spontaneously. The group consulted White three or four times. Whenever White thought he had one toy "figured out" he would move on to another. For demonstration, each selected the toys he or she wanted to demonstrate with a minimum of bickering and competition. White came to the rescue of others when they were unable to explain; he also took some of the refused or neglected toys and demonstrated and explained them. No organization, formal or informal, was achieved, but Red and Blue assumed most responsibility for the goal-orientation of the group. The two girls manifested considerable "out of their field" behavior and disclaimed "knowing anything about things like this." The group initiated 29 ideas, demonstrated 30, and explained 22, a performance that won first place. Agreement on relative merit of contributions was statistically significant (<.01), giving the following order: Red, White, Blue, Green, and Gold.

In summary, the tendency for the most creative group member to work silently and alone persisted into the fourth grade. The other members tended to pair off and shift spontaneously from one pairing to another. In most of the groups, the second most creative member became a goal-oriented leader and the most creative seemed glad to accept this domination. The most creative children tended to let others dominate the procedures, filling in the gaps of the group's performance when others faltered or when the rest of the group ran out of ideas. Four or five of the most creative initiated the most ideas in their groups but none of them was rated as making the most valuable contribution, this honor usually going to the second most creative.

Fifth-Grade Groups. In the first group, each member immediately took a toy and examined it without saying much. Gold tended to play and distract the goal-orientation. White busied herself by writing down her ideas but was not very verbal at first. During the exploratory period, however, she initiated a larger number of ideas than anyone else and all were of a goal-oriented nature. Although White seemed to have no interest in leadership, she assumed leadership roles when this became necessary for the functioning of the group and her suggestions were readily accepted. Although there was no real organization, there was considerable interaction among members, and groups tended to function for the most part as groups. Agreement on the relative importance of contributions was not statistically significant, but the following order resulted: Green, White, Red, and Gold. The group initiated 17 ideas, demonstrated 13, and explained 9, winning third place.

In the second group, Gold picked up the sparkler and everyone talked about it and manipulated it. The group systematically took one toy at a time, formed hypotheses about it, and tested them. White participated actively, gradually becoming more aggressive. She succeeded in getting most of her ideas accepted and helped assign toys for the demonstration. She made certain that Blue was included and could explain her toys. Unusual in that it consistently formed hypotheses and proceeded to test them, this group initiated 50 ideas, demonstrated 11, and explained 6, ranking fifth. Agreement concerning merit of contributions was statistically significant (<.01), the following order resulting: White, Gold, Red, and Blue.

The third group was enthusiastic but generally lacking in real ideas. Although Blue was dominant, the group was more receptive to Green.

White and Green formed a coalition against Blue. The group initiated 30 ideas, demonstrated 17, but explained only three correctly. This performance placed the group in fourth place. There was little consensus on the relative value of contributions, the following order resulting: Green, Red, Blue, and White.

At the outset, then, each member of the fourth group immediately grabbed a toy and began to manipulate it. White, quiet and unassertive, was occasionally consulted by other group members. She was almost last in the volunteer order, never pushing her ideas and frequently depreciating their worth. Agreement concerning relative merit of contributions was statistically significant ($<.01$), the following order being derived: Red, Green, Blue, Gold, and White. The group initiated 47 ideas, demonstrated 16, and explained 10, placing second.

Action in the fifth group was fast and furious, primarily because of the aggressiveness and the driving but imaginative leadership of White. He dominated by sheer force of personality and brilliance, although Red gave him a good fight and was not in the least daunted. Green, a girl, made little effort. Blue kept in the fight but no one paid him much attention except Green. White told everyone what to do and definitely tried to direct and motivate the group. Red several times attacked White, telling him that he was "too scientific." White was also criticized for being too greedy in dividing the toys for the demonstration. Near the end, White showed a budding sensitivity and tried to draw Green into the activity through a joint demonstration with him. A high degree of consensus ($<.01$) concerning relative value of contributions resulted in the following order: White, Red, a tie between Blue and Green. The group initiated 32 ideas, demonstrated 44, and explained 34, placing it far out front in the competition.

In these fifth-grade groups, strategies in handling the most creative members and their counterstrategies were more differentiated and varied than in the lower grades. The older groups tended to use organization to a greater extent and to respond more to leadership, although they still represented to a considerable degree a primitive battle of egos. Two of the five most creative were ranked by their peers as making the most valuable contribution to their group's success. Three initiated the most ideas in their respective groups.

Sixth-Grade Groups. The first of the sixth-grade groups was sparked from beginning to end by an aggressive, irrepressible, highly creative boy. He spontaneously assumed leadership but did not tie himself down with paperwork or formal administrative processes. He appointed Gold, a girl, to record everyone's ideas, much to her dislike. The action moved so fast and so many ideas were flowing, however, that it would have been impossible for her to have recorded them all. White did, however, consult Gold's notes before the beginning of the demonstration. Throughout the exploratory period White ran about the room, spouting off ideas in an almost continuous flow, occasionally answering the questions of other members. Although the other members were somewhat overwhelmed and unable to cope with White's productivity, all of them remained in the struggle. Green commented during the exploratory period that the group would lose because no one would listen to his ideas. Not until the demonstration was well underway did the other members become really irritated with White's domination and his giving them little or no opportunity to present their ideas. When a coalition of Green and Gold attacked him, he acquiesced momentarily, but after about thirty seconds he resumed his flow of ideas. Because of its fast and furious pace, particularly that of White, this was by far the most productive of the sixth-grade groups. The group initiated 67 ideas, demonstrated 35, and explained 33. The degree of consensus concerning the relative value of contributions was statistically significant (Kendall's $\omega = .60$, significant at about the .05 level). All agreed that White made the most valuable contribution. In rating himself first, White commented, "I hate to be so bigheaded, but . . ." The others tied for the remaining positions.

In the second group, White, a girl, was at first aggressively dominant and directive. Immediately upon sensing hostility from the group she resorted to "clowning around," apparently to atone for her earlier bossiness and to prove herself one of the gang. Without a dominating leader the group then floundered for a while, and finally Gold, a boy, assumed a goal-oriented leadership role and was recognized as making the most valuable contribution to the group's success. White assigned positions in the order for presenting demonstrations by writing a number on each member's arm band. Agreement on the relative value of contributions was statistically significant (Kendall's $\omega = .62$, significant at the .01 level). The following order resulted: Gold, White, Green, Blue, and Red. The group initiated 38 ideas, demonstrated 34, and explained 25, placing second.

The third group achieved little organization. At first all were eager and talked at the same time. White at first wanted everyone to listen to her ideas but the group did not respond positively. After having her ideas ignored or rejected, White became preoccupied and tossed in an idea only occasionally, but still amassed the largest number of ideas initiated. Red was the real organizer. Consensus on the relative importance of contributions was statistically significant (Kendall's $\omega = .66$, significant at the .01 level), producing the following order: Red, Blue, Green, White, and Gold. The group initiated 27 ideas, demonstrated 18, and explained 16, placing fourth in the standings.

The fourth group immediately appointed Gold as chairman and Green as secretary. Each member was assigned a toy. White, a girl, was reprimanded for trying to work out of turn. Near the end of the exploratory phase, she was assigned several difficult toys to explain and her explanations were accepted and used by others in the demonstration. White was assigned only one toy to demonstrate and explain in the final phase. Gold dominated the group, hitchhiked on the ideas of others, and gave good explanations. The group's functioning was orderly owing to the strong leadership of Gold, who overruled White when she continued to try to make suggestions. All agreed that Gold made the most valuable contribution to the group's success. Green, White, Red, and Blue followed in order. The group initiated 28 ideas, demonstrated 15, and explained 12, placing fifth in the standings. White managed to initiate the largest number of ideas but was permitted to demonstrate only one principle in the final stage.

At the outset, the others all recognized White's talent and appointed him chairman and recorder. One said, "White is our brain boy." Another said, "White is our genius; let's let him figure it out." Another said, "White can remember best." Saddled with the paperwork and administrative responsibility, White was unable to manipulate the toys and had to devote himself to processing the ideas of others and to keeping order. He assumed the responsibility for demonstrating and explaining the toys rejected by others. The degree of agreement on the relative merit of contributions was statistically significant (Kendall's $\omega = .64$, significant at the .01 level). Final rankings were as follows: White, Gold, Green, Red, and Blue. The group initiated 40 ideas, demonstrated 21, and explained 18, placing third.

Further inspection of the data reveals that the most creative member initiated the largest number of ideas in four of the five groups. The exception occurred in the fifth group, where the most creative member was assigned the role of chairman and recorder; he compensated, however, by presenting and explaining a larger number of principles than any of the other members. In four of the five groups, the most creative member presented and explained the most principles. The exception occurred in the fourth group, where the most creative member was assigned only one toy, nutty putty, to demonstrate. In only two cases was the most creative member voted as making the most valuable contribution. Agreement concerning the rankings was high in all the sixth-grade groups, however.

In summary, the individualized and differentiated strategies that emerged in the fifth-grade groups became more distinct and dramatic in the sixth-grade groups. Organization seems to have become far more important as a technique of controlling the most creative group member. Only in the first group did the most creative member triumph over organization, seizing the initiative and refusing to be suppressed by group pressures; organization, paperwork, and procedure tended to melt in the face of such productivity. His domination, however, seemed to be an expression of productivity and goal-orientation, not of a desire for power. Although the first group attempted to control the most creative member by aggressive attack, he was too irrepressible to be intimidated by their aggressiveness and hostility. In the second group the most creative member seized the initiative also, but apparently began to feel guilty about her dominance on sensing the displeasure of the others and responded to this pressure by clowning around to regain the good graces of the group. In the third group the other members controlled the most creative member by ignoring and rejecting her ideas. In response, she became preoccupied and contributed only sporadically to the group task. In the fourth group formal organization was used to control the most creative member. First, stern reprimands were tried, and finally sanctions were exercised in the form of limiting her activities by giving her only one toy to demonstrate and explain. In the fifth group the most creative member was held in check by loading him with the paperwork and administrative responsibility. He responded by accepting these responsibilities and contributed creatively only when others faltered in their explanations or when they had exhausted their ideas.

DISCUSSION

Although the sample in this experiment is extremely narrow and the experiment needs to be replicated in several elementary schools of different types, the results provide potentially useful insights into the strategies used by groups to control their most creative members and the counterstrategies used by the latter. The behavior of these groups of elementary school children mirrors many of the problems experienced by adult groups in dealing with their most creative members.

In the second grade we have perhaps the most primitive level of group behavior. There is a lack of group identification; everyone works for himself alone. The uniformly unpleasant behavior of the most creative members suggests the need for teachers and parents to help highly creative children develop less obnoxious techniques for presenting their ideas and getting them accepted during the earliest school years. At this level, the most creative members are themselves responsible for much of their difficulty.

From the second through the sixth grade there is a decreasing tendency to engage in individual manipulation and in the development of ideas and an increasing tendency to become more organized. From the data available, it is difficult to determine the extent to which the tendency to work alone which persists fairly well through the fourth grade should be discouraged. Plainly, the tendency of organization to control the most creative tends to coerce some highly creative children and to reduce severely their usefulness. There are, of course, the aggressive, irrepressible subjects like the most creative members in the first of the sixth-grade groups and the fifth of the fifth-grade groups. There are also diplomatic, creative persons who feel their way gradually, and slowly win acceptance of their ideas, as with the most creative in the second of the fifth-grade groups. That creative people should be required to expend so much energy in "being nice" in order to obtain a hearing for their ideas is regrettable.

Highly interesting in reference to the problem of rewarding the most creative members in adult groups is the behavior of the fifth of the sixth-grade groups. A group frequently exalts its most creative member by placing him in an administrative or power position. Research thus far (Compton, 1953) indicates an absence of the desire for power among our creative scientists. Perhaps it is damaging to put our most creative and productive scientists and teachers in administrative positions. Many of them would prefer positions more closely related to their real interests. Usually, they are forced to devote their time to endless paperwork and the processing of inferior ideas developed by subordinates. Weighted down, they are unable to engage in the manipulation of materials and ideas that results in creative productivity. Either they are limited in opportunity to exercise their creativity or they neglect their administrative responsibilities and the enterprise bogs down from lack of proper direction and support. Yet in government service, in industry, and in education, the highest rewards almost always go to the administrator rather than to the outstanding creative researcher, teacher, or engineer. Perhaps our society needs to become more imaginative in seeking better ways of rewarding creative achievement.

It is interesting to compare the behavior of the most creative children in the contrived groups of this study with that reported in a similar study by Merei (1949) of subjects highly talented in leadership. In

Merei's study the children with high abilities in leadership were introduced into small groups already functioning as groups and having established traditions. In the overwhelming majority of Merei's groups, the
newcomer had to accept the group's traditions but still managed to play
the role of leader. Some accomplished this by giving orders, some by
taking possession of the toys and objects in the room, and others by
exercising diplomacy. Few of our most creative subjects displayed either
the willingness to accept the group's way of doing things or the desire
for power displayed by Merei's little leaders. A few of the most creative
dominated by virtue of their outstanding productivity alone, apparently motivated by the need to open a channel for the expression of their
ideas.

SUMMARY

The objective of this exploratory study was to generate ideas about
the sanctions exercised by groups against their most creative members,
the techniques used to hold the creative in check, and the counterstrategies of the highly creative in coping with peer sanctions and organizational pressures.

One class at each grade level from second through sixth grade was
divided into five groups of five persons each and confronted with the
task of discovering what principles can be demonstrated and explained
with a collection of science toys. Groups were composed on the basis of
scores obtained on a test of creative thinking administered earlier, with
one of the five most creative members being placed in each group. The
focus of observation was on the techniques used by the group to control
the most creative member and his method of adaptation. Groups were
given twenty-five minutes in which to examine and manipulate the toys
in an attempt to discover what can be done with them and why they
work as they do. They were then given five minutes in which to organize
their demonstrations and twenty-five minutes for the demonstrations.
A prize was awarded to the group in each class which demonstrated and
explained the largest number of principles.

Rather clear evidence of pressure against the most creative member
was found in each of the twenty-five groups studied. A majority (68 per
cent) of the most creative initiated more ideas than any other member
of the group, just as they did in the test of creativity administered earlier. Few (24 per cent) were credited by the other members with making
the most valuable contribution to the group's performance. Boys tended
to demonstrate and explain more principles than girls. At the fifth-grade
level, however, the girls initiated slightly more ideas than the boys, an

accomplishment compatible with what appears to be a spurt in the development of creative thinking abilities in girls at the fifth-grade level.

From second through sixth grade we find a decreasing tendency for group members to work alone, especially the most creative ones, rather than as a part of a group. The tendency for the most creative to work alone rather strongly persists through the fifth grade, at which point the tendency for groups to organize begins to emerge as an important technique in controlling the most creative members. By the sixth grade, groups have developed a varied repertoire of controls. The most creative have in turn developed a varied repertoire of techniques of adaptation. Techniques of control include open aggression and hostility, criticism, rejection and/or indifference, the use of organizational machinery to limit scope of operation and to impose sanctions, and exaltation to a position of power involving paperwork and administrative responsibility. Adaptation techniques of the most creative members include compliance, counteraggressiveness, indomitable persistence, apparent ignoring of criticism, clowning, silence and apathy or preoccupation, inconsistent performance, filling the gaps when others falter, and solitary activity. These categories need to be expanded by studying groups in elementary schools having different types of population.

EVOKING CREATIVE THINKING IN THE PRIMARY GRADES

MANY methods are being offered for evoking more and better creative ideas from individuals and groups. A few of these methods are being evaluated objectively through controlled experiments, though reports have been limited to research with adult groups. The experiment reported here was undertaken to encourage creative thinking among young children.

Osborn has suggested a set of questions or principles for stimulating new ideas. Though useful in a variety of situations, these questions are most directly applicable in developing ideas for improving a product, a procedure, or a group performance. We used them to stimulate children to think of ideas for improving a toy:

What would happen if we made it larger? (Magnification)
What would happen if we made it smaller? (Minification)
What could we add? (Addition)
What would happen if we took something away? (Subtraction)
What would happen if we took something away and put something else in its place? (Substitution)
What would happen if we took it apart? (Division)
How could we rearrange it? (Rearrangement)
What would happen if we multiplied it? (Pairs, sets, etc.) (Multiplication)
What would happen if we changed its position? (Reversal)
What would happen if we made it out of a different kind of material? (Material)
What would happen if we gave it motion? (Sensory appeal: motion)
What would happen if we gave it odor? (Odor)
What would happen if we gave it light? (Light)
What would happen if we gave it sound? (Sound)
What would happen if we changed the color? (Color)

NOTE: This chapter was originally published in *The Elementary School Journal* (October 1961, pp. 34–41), with whose permission it is reprinted here.

What would happen if we changed the shape? (Shape)
What would happen if we made it stronger? (Adaptation)
What would happen if we put it to other uses? (Other uses)

The first objective of our experiment was to determine whether children in the primary grades can be taught to use these questions.

Our second objective was to compare the effects of two approaches. In the first, we instructed children to think of as many ideas as possible without attention to the quality of the ideas. In the second, we urged the children to think of the most interesting, the most clever, the most unusual ideas they could.

Motivation to produce a large number of ideas has had an important place in training programs designed to help individuals and groups develop new ideas. Osborn (1957) and others contend that the more ideas produced, the greater the chances of obtaining "good ideas."

The subjects of our experiment were 375 pupils enrolled in Grades 1 through 3 in two elementary schools — 204 pupils in School X and 171 pupils in School Y. All the pupils in two classrooms in each of the three grades in each school were included in the experiment.

The pupils in each classroom of School X were randomly divided into four groups:

Group A was trained and motivated to produce as many ideas as possible.

Group B was trained and motivated to produce quality ideas.

Group C was not trained but was motivated to produce as many ideas as possible.

Group D was not trained but was motivated to produce quality ideas.

All subjects in School Y were administered the same creative thinking task as the subjects in School X but did not receive the training and the specific instructions for quantity and quality of ideas.

TRAINING PROCEDURE

In each class in School X, Groups A and B meeting together were asked to develop ideas for improving a toy fire truck to make it "more fun for boys and girls to play with." The children's ideas were simply acknowledged with some indication of interest by the experimenter.

Then the experimenter set out to apply Osborn's questions, or principles, by means of a set of squares that had been modified according to the principles, as illustrated in Figure 14.

The experimenter showed the squares one at a time to the children.

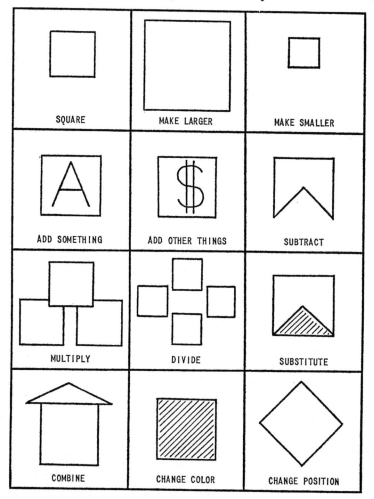

Figure 14. Modifications of square to illustrate principles for developing new ideas.

As each square was held up, the experimenter asked: "What have I done to the square here?"

The principle illustrated was then related to the suggestions the children had made for improving the toy fire truck. Most groups suggested adding something to the fire truck — a hose, a first-aid kit, and top lights. When the children identified the principles of addition illustrated by the squares, the examiner would say, "Yes, you remember you suggested adding a hose and a first-aid kit to the fire truck."

If any of the principles were not illustrated by the children's responses, the group was asked to supply the deficiency. For example, if no one had offered suggestions illustrating the principle of combination, the experimenter would hold up the appropriate square and say, "I don't believe you suggested one for the fire truck like this. What could you put with the fire truck?" The children would then respond: "A fire house." "A board with a play town." "A fire hydrant." "A cardboard house in flames."

Finally the children were told that the questions could be used in "thinking up ideas about almost anything."

All training sessions were conducted by the author. Each session lasted about twenty minutes.

TESTING PROCEDURE

Each subject was tested individually by a member of the staff of the Bureau of Educational Research, all of whom had had extensive experience in testing children with the type of task used.

The test task required the children to think of ideas for improving a stuffed toy dog. Each child was allowed eight minutes to dictate his ideas to the examiner. The time used in giving instructions was not counted in the eight minutes.

Groups A and C were instructed as follows: "How many ideas can you think of to improve this little toy dog (handing toy to child) so boys and girls will have more fun playing with it? I'll try to write them down just as fast as you can tell them to me. Tell me every idea you can think of; it doesn't matter how good it is or how crazy it sounds. Don't worry about how much it would cost."

Groups B and D were asked: "What interesting, clever, and unusual ideas can you think of to improve this little toy dog (handing toy to child) so boys and girls will have more fun playing with it? I'll try to write them down just as fast as you tell them to me. Think of as exciting ideas as you can. Don't worry about how much it would cost."

An attempt was made to maintain motivation by offering a prize for the best performance in each group in each grade.

Children in Groups C and D were tested in separate rooms immediately after the experiment was explained to the entire class and the groups were formed. Children in Groups A and B were tested immediately after the training session described earlier.

Responses to the test task were scored on the basis of the number of ideas given (fluency), the number of principles or approaches used (flexibility), and the number of clever or unusual ideas offered. The scoring was done according to instructions in a previously developed manual. An interscorer reliability of .93 was obtained between two judges, who followed the manual.

To illustrate the scoring procedure, let us take six responses from the record of one boy in third grade who suggested the following improvements for the toy dog: (1) Give him feet that would go round so that as he moves he would dig a hole. (2) Make his tail longer. (3) Put a hero medal on him or a medal he won at a dog show. (4) Put a tiny tape recorder inside him so that what you say is recorded in dog language so he can answer you. (5) Put fleas on him — or flies. (6) Hook him up so that he can drink water from a bowl and so it will run down through a little tube and run back in the bowl and won't mess things up.

Each response received a point for fluency (score: 6). The first response illustrates the principle of "giving sensory appeal" (motion); the second, "magnification"; the third, "addition"; the fourth, "addition"; the fifth, "addition"; and the sixth, "combination." The boy therefore received a score of 3 on flexibility. Only the second response, which was given by a high percentage of the children, was not judged to have qualities of cleverness. Consequently, he received a score of 5 on cleverness.

RESULTS

The data on the toy-improvement task are presented in Tables 15 and 16. General trends for the four conditions at the various grade levels are shown in Figure 15, which summarizes the data on total scores. The curves for the two trained groups are consistently above those for the two untrained groups. The curve for the trained groups that were urged to give interesting, unusual, and clever ideas is consistently above the curve for the other groups in each grade.

A two-way analysis of variance was performed to determine whether the observed effects of training and motivation can be accepted with confidence. The results show that the effects of training are statistically significant at better than the 5 per cent level of confidence for the second and third grades but not for the first. These results hold for all scores: fluency (number of ideas), flexibility (number of approaches), cleverness, and total.

The children who were asked to think of as many ideas as possible without regard to quality showed a consistent tendency to give fewer responses than the children who were asked to think of clever, interesting, and unusual ideas. The results are statistically significant only in the second grade, however.

Scores obtained by children in School Y were compared with those

Table 15. Mean Scores and Standard Deviations for Four Experimental Conditions on a Toy-Improvement Test of Creative Thinking

Grade and Condition*	Pupils	Fluency		Flexibility		Cleverness	
		Mean	S.D.†	Mean	S.D.†	Mean	S.D.†
First grade							
Group A	18	12.61	4.60	5.50	1.95	5.89	2.85
Group B	15	14.07	6.95	5.33	2.80	6.80	5.52
Group C	19	11.11	6.66	4.32	2.03	5.32	5.17
Group D	16	11.31	6.45	4.62	2.06	6.19	4.11
Second grade							
Group A	20	14.15	6.04	5.90	2.10	6.15	4.29
Group B	17	20.35	8.66	7.53	2.85	11.29	6.26
Group C	21	10.00	5.19	3.52	1.68	3.81	4.26
Group D	17	11.59	5.94	4.12	2.61	5.47	4.23
Third grade							
Group A	18	16.56	6.26	6.56	2.03	10.61	4.82
Group B	11	21.18	5.88	8.18	1.53	13.09	4.01
Group C	19	16.68	9.23	5.53	2.23	8.47	6.89
Group D	13	14.46	6.23	5.62	1.69	6.15	4.85

* Group A: trained, motivated to produce large number of responses; Group B: trained, motivated to produce clever, unusual responses; Group C: untrained, motivated to produce large number of responses; Group D: untrained, motivated to produce clever, unusual responses.

† According to Bartlett's test, the variance is not significant at the 5 per cent level of confidence for any of the grades for any of the measures.

Table 16. Total Mean Scores and Standard Deviations on a Toy-Improvement Test of Creative Thinking

Grade and Condition	No. of Pupils	Mean	S.D.*
First grade			
Group A	18	24.00	7.37
Group B	15	26.20	14.23
Group C	19	20.75	12.85
Group D	16	22.12	11.44
Second grade			
Group A	20	26.20	11.16
Group B	17	39.17	16.52
Group C	21	17.33	9.98
Group D	17	21.18	11.41
Third grade			
Group A	18	33.73	11.22
Group B	11	42.45	9.32
Group C	19	30.68	17.36
Group D	13	26.23	11.42

* According to Bartlett's test, the variance is not significant at the 5 per cent level of confidence in any of the grades for any of the measures.

achieved by the untrained subjects (Groups C and D) in School X. No statistically significant differences were found in the average scores for any grade. Since other data available indicate that there were no differences in the quality of the pupils enrolled in these two schools, this result suggests that the differences found in the basic experiment were owing

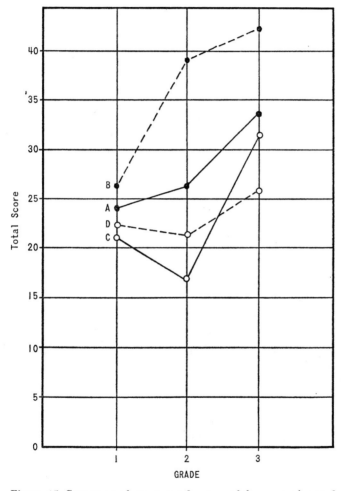

Figure 15. Summary of mean total scores of four experimental conditions by grades (A: trained, motivated to produce a large number of responses. B: trained, motivated to produce clever, unusual responses. C: untrained, motivated to produce a large number of responses. D: untrained, motivated to produce clever, unusual responses.).

to the teaching of the principles and the motivation rather than to the warm-up and practice.

Except in the first grade, the children who had the benefit of the training procedures described in this experiment produced more ideas and showed more flexibility and more cleverness in their thinking than the children who had no training.

In the first-grade groups, the experimenter noted difficulty in getting the children to follow the training program during the stage when principles were developed. All first-grade groups were active and productive during the first stage of the training session; but during the second phase interest seemed to diminish, and there were interchanges within the group. A more effective technique or a more effective experimenter might have produced more favorable results. Probably too many concepts were presented in too short a time, or perhaps by the second phase the children were tired.

Perhaps the most surprising finding of the study is that instructions to produce a large number of ideas without regard for quality produced fewer responses than did admonitions to produce clever, interesting, and unusual ideas. One would guess that instructions to think of "clever, interesting, and unusual ideas" tended to free the child for responses more than the admonition to think of as many ideas as possible, without bothering about "how good they are." If subjects had been threatened with penalties for "poor ideas" or instructed to give "only good, sound ideas," the results might have been different.

Since the training and the testing were both concerned with the improvement of a product, in this case a toy, it cannot be determined from this study whether the procedures used would be effective in training persons to produce ideas for improving processes, situations, and interpersonal relations. It is quite likely, however, that the applicability is broad.

CONCLUSION

Results of this experiment indicate that pupils in the primary grades, with the possible exception of the first grade, can in a short period be taught a set of principles that will enable them to produce more and better ideas than they would have without training. The results provide no support for motivating pupils in the primary grades to produce a quantity of ideas without consideration for quality.

CHANGING REACTIONS OF PREADOLESCENT GIRLS
TO SCIENCE TASKS

It is well known that extremely few women have achieved eminence as scientific discoverers or inventors. Experiments such as the ones described in the preceding reports show that in the early school years girls develop attitudes, interests, and even disabilities that make it difficult for them to become scientific discoverers and inventors. Moreover, these trends are so strong as to suggest that the attitudes of girls in today's elementary schools make difficult a healthy adjustment in our culture.

In an experiment involving the use of science toys, many girls in the fourth through sixth grades shrank from participation. The experimenters frequently heard the comment, "I'm a girl. I'm not supposed to know anything about science." As a result, the performance of boys was significantly superior to that of girls on this task. In an individual test of product improvement, using common toys, boys achieved superiority over girls by the second grade and increased it in the third.

About thirteen months after the original study involving science toys was completed, it was replicated in the fourth, fifth, and sixth grades with an alternate set of materials. During the experiment it became quite obvious that the attitudes of the girls toward tasks requiring creative scientific thinking had changed significantly since the original study. The purpose of this report is to present and analyze some of the objective data collected and to attempt to determine the degree and nature of the observed changes in attitude and behavior.

PROCEDURES

Subjects. The subjects of the study were the pupils enrolled in the fourth, fifth, and sixth grades of a university elementary school during two school years, 1958–59 and 1959–60. Twenty-five children were enrolled in each grade and were divided into five groups of five members each. In a few groups one member was absent at the time of the experiment, but no group consisted of less than four members. In both years, the study was conducted during the spring quarter near the end of the school year (April in 1959 and May in 1960).

In 1959, 34 boys and 36 girls participated; in 1960, there were 32 boys and 38 girls. The proportion of boys and girls was about the same in all classes and an effort was made to keep the ratio 2:3 or 3:2 in each group. Although there is a wide range of ability among the children enrolled in this school, there is a disproportionately large number of high ability children and children from professional families.

Experimental Procedures. In each class, all five groups were tested simultaneously, each in a different room under a trained experimenter. In an attempt to maximize motivation, prizes of interesting science books were offered for the best group or team performance. In the orientation, the terms "group" and "team" were emphasized. To simplify the recording of observations and the reporting of results, each subject was given a colored arm band, by which color the observations recorded were distinguished.

Each group was provided a box of science toys and toy parts. In 1959, Science Toy Collection Number 2 of the Library of Science (59 Fourth Avenue, New York 3, N.Y.) was used. This collection includes a sparkler, a finger trap, a pin trick, a four-ball puzzle, a topsy-turvy top, a jumping top, a blow ball, a flying saucer, and nutty putty. To this collection were added a magnifying glass, a magnet, and a whistle. In 1960, Science Toy Collection Number 3 was used, which includes a bang gun, a string telephone, a siren, a busy bee, a calliope whistle, a cat cry, a tower of Hanoi puzzle, a secret, a Nim game, a square puzzle, a something-for-nothing puzzle, and a tetrahedron puzzle. A magnet and a magnifying glass were also included.

Each group was given twenty-five minutes in which to explore and experiment to discover what could be done with the toys and toy parts and to determine why they function as they do. It was emphasized that in addition to figuring out what each toy was intended to do they should try to think of other uses. Five minutes were then allotted for planning and organizing the demonstrations and explanations. The group then demonstrated and explained the principles they had figured out. The time limit was twenty-five minutes. Finally, each subject was asked to rank each member of his group according to the value of his contribution to the group's success. In addition, in 1960, subjects were asked how well they enjoyed the activity and how well they thought their group would compare with the other four groups.

The experimenters tabulated on a specially prepared record sheet the number of ideas initiated by each subject during the exploratory phase and recorded all the ideas demonstrated and explained during the subsequent phase. In addition, observations were made on how the group organized itself and got underway, on how the members grouped themselves during the exploratory period, on the general activity level, on the roles developed by specific members, and on how the group planned the demonstrations.

RESULTS

In 1959, boys were far ahead of girls on ideas demonstrated and on scientific principles explained, averaging 6.18 and 4.65 respectively, compared with 3.06 and 1.78 for girls. In 1960 the means for boys and girls were almost identical, 4.47 and 2.33 for boys and 4.34 and 2.11 for girls.

The analysis of variance data to test the significance of the observed differences in means is presented in Table 17. On ideas demonstrated and principles explained there is no significant effect owing to year but there are significant effects owing to sex and interaction. Girls tended to go up and boys tended to go down on both of these measures.

We can now test the differences in means for boys and girls separately for each of the two years. These tests are presented in Table 18. In 1959 boys demonstrated significantly more ideas and explained significantly more scientific principles than girls. For 1960, however, the performance of girls does not differ significantly from that of boys.

Since girls contributed as much to the scores of their groups as boys, it is of interest to know whether their contribution to the success of their groups was valued to the same extent as that of boys. Composite ranks were determined by adding the individual rankings and then ranking the totals. Table 19 presents a comparison of the composite rankings of girls and boys for each of the two years. In both years the contributions of boys are more highly valued than those of girls. No significant change occurs in the rankings of boys or of girls between 1959 and 1960.

In 1959 many of the girls did not enjoy participation in the experiment and protested that it was not an appropriate activity for girls. In 1960 each subject was asked to indicate how much he enjoyed or disliked participation in the experiment. Responses were made on a five-point scale but only one subject (a boy) used the dislike end of the scale. Girls reported as much enjoyment of the activity as boys. In fact, what little difference there is favors girls.

It is also important to know how boys and girls value their own contribution. The rankings made in both 1959 and 1960 required subjects to include themselves (except in one group in 1959 when one experi-

Table 17. Analysis of Variance Data to Test Significance of Sex and
Year Differences in Performance on the Science-Toy Task
among Pupils in Grades Four through Six

Source of Variance	Degree of Freedom	Mean Square	F-ratio	P
Ideas Demonstrated				
Year	1	0.3491	0.35	n.s.
Sex	1	93.7293	9.11	<.01
Interaction	1	76.8551	7.47	<.01
Error	136	10.2898		
Principles Explained				
Year	1	27.5979	3.28	n.s.
Sex	1	85.1226	10.11	<.01
Interaction	1	59.7176	7.09	<.01
Error	136	8.4195		

Table 18. Tests of Significance of Differences in Means for Boys and Girls in 1959 and
1960 on Performance Variables of Science-Toy Task

Mean (1959)				Mean (1960)			
Boys	Girls	F-ratio	P	Boys	Girls	F-ratio	P
Ideas Demonstrated							
6.18	3.06	13.09	<.01	4.47	4.34	0.03	n.s.
Principles Explained							
4.65	1.78	11.38	<.01	2.33	2.11	0.21	n.s.

Table 19. Comparison of Composite Rankings in Five-Person Groups
of Boys and Girls for Value of Contribution to Success of
Group on Scientific-Toy Task in 1959 and 1960 *

Composite Ranking	1959		1960	
	Boys	Girls	Boys	Girls
First	13	2	11	3
Second	6	7	7	7
Third	7	10	6	10
Fourth	4	11	2	15
Fifth	4	5	4	3

* In some groups there were ties; in others one absent member
was not ranked.

NOTE: χ^2 (Boys 1959 vs. Girls 1959) = 12.04; $P < .01$
χ^2 (Boys 1960 vs. Girls 1960) = 14.92; $P < .01$
χ^2 (Boys 1959 vs. Boys 1960) = 0.74; n.s.
χ^2 (Girls 1959 vs. Girls 1960) = 1.20; n.s.

menter failed to obtain this information). Comparison of the self-rankings of boys with those of girls for the two years by means of chi-squares shows a consistent but not quite statistically significant tendency ($p \cong$ .10) over the two years for boys to value their contribution to their group's success more highly than girls value theirs.

DISCUSSION

The reactions of fourth, fifth, and sixth grade girls in the elementary school studied, changed in significant and important ways during the period between April 1959 and May 1960. In 1959, boys demonstrated more ideas and explained more scientific principles than girls. In 1960, in the same school, girls demonstrated as many ideas and explained as many principles as boys. In 1959, many girls expressed obvious dislike for the science-toy task and tended to withdraw from active participation in it. In 1960, none of this dislike was observed. In fact, girls reported as much enjoyment of the task as boys did.

One aspect of the situation, however, has not changed. The contribution of boys to the success of the group continues to be evaluated more highly than that of girls. There is also a slight and almost significant trend for boys to evaluate their own contributions to the success of their groups more highly than do girls. In other words, cultural and/or subcultural changes seem to be making it more permissible for girls to participate in and enjoy tasks requiring creative scientific thinking, but the contributions of boys are still more highly valued by their peers than those of girls.

To help us better understand the reasons for these changes, we need only remind ourselves of two contributory factors. First, during the period in which the data were collected, national interest had been focused on the need for identifying and developing creative scientific talent. There is little doubt in my mind that between 1959 and 1960 the general attitude toward science and scientists was becoming more and more favorable. Second, the results of earlier studies of the influence of sex differences in creative thinking, results which I discussed in 1959 with the parents and teachers of the subjects in the present study, also played a part in effecting the changes recorded in 1960. These studies had shown that misplaced emphasis or overemphasis on sex roles during the early school years interferes with the development of the creative thinking abilities, a point I stressed in my talks with the parents and teachers.

Cultural emphasis on sex roles is a source of many conflicts for highly creative persons and actually interferes with school learning and with the full development of the creative potential in children. The high degree of sensitivity that is a part of creative thinking has a distinctly feminine character in our society, while at the same time the independence required by creative thinking has a distinctly masculine character. The highly creative boy is likely to appear more effeminate than other boys his age and the highly creative girl is likely to appear more masculine than other girls her age. Unfortunately, social sanctions against such development may cause many children to sacrifice their creativity at an early age.

In my talks with parents and teachers, I maintained that parents must recognize that even though they might not want their girls to participate in the tasks of invention and scientific discovery, girls will still need to know much about the physical world. Both boys and girls should be encouraged to talk, ask questions, seek answers, and experiment. No discrimination between boys and girls should enter into the explanations given them about how things work. That girls should be taught to be as accurate and keen in their observations as boys, that their questions should be taken as seriously as those asked by their brothers, need not in any way interfere with the boy's learning to be a man and the girl's learning to be a woman.

SUMMARY

In 1959 and again in 1960 a small-group task requiring creative scientific thinking was administered in the fourth, fifth, and sixth grades of a university elementary school. Alternate sets of science toys were used for the task and the experiments were conducted at approximately the same time of year (April in 1959 and May in 1960). The twenty-five members of each class were divided into five five-person groups and each group was tested in a separate room. Twenty-five minutes was allowed for experimentation and exploration, during which observations were made about the initiation of ideas. After a five-minute planning period, twenty-five minutes was allowed for demonstrations and explanations of scientific principles. During this period observations were made about the number of ideas demonstrated and the number of principles correctly explained. At the end, subjects were asked to rank each member of the group, including themselves, on the basis of the value of their contribution to the group's success. In 1960 data were obtained on enjoyment of the tasks.

The results show that significant changes took place between 1959 and 1960 in the performance of girls on this task. In 1959, boys demonstrated and explained a significantly greater number of principles than girls. In 1960 the performance of girls equaled that of boys. The contributions of boys, however, continued to be valued more highly by the groups than those of girls, although girls reported as much enjoyment of the task as boys. The tendency of boys to evaluate their own performance more highly than girls is consistent but does not quite reach statistical significance.

SEX-ROLE IDENTIFICATION AND CREATIVITY

THIS exploratory study was suggested by a variety of research findings derived from recent studies of creativity, including those of the author (Torrance, 1961a). The most immediate stimulus was a suggestion by Anne Roe (1959) at the Third National Conference on the Identification of Creative Scientific Talent. In discussing the personal problems of creative scientists, she listed as one of the more persistent the difficulty of sex-role identification in the highly creative person. She pointed out that, on measures of masculinity-femininity, the highly creative person of either sex is likely to be higher on the scale of the opposite sex than less creative peers of his own sex. As she explains, the high degree of sensitivity required for creative work is a distinctly feminine characteristic in our culture, whereas the independence and dominance required is of definite masculine character.

Both sensitivity and independence have frequently been revealed as the characteristics that differentiate the highly creative from the less creative members in a given group. In a study of the characteristics of the more creative students in a mental hygiene course, we found that the more creative members had stronger needs for dominance and ego achievement (masculine characteristics) and stronger needs for nurturance, affiliation, and succorance (feminine characteristics) than the less creative members of the group as measured by the Stern Activities Index (Torrance et al., 1958). Stein (1956) has shown that the more highly creative research chemists are more autonomous and more self-confident than the less creative ones. At the same time, Stein's more creative subjects are described as allowing their hypotheses to be generated from within the problem rather than attempting to superimpose hypotheses onto it prematurely, suggesting a high degree of sensitivity. Drevdahl (1954) found that the more creative advanced students as identified by instructors were more self-sufficient and held more radical social views than less creative students in the same fields. Cattell and Drevdahl (1955) found a high degree of both dominance and sensitivity among eminent researchers.

In a study of one hundred Air Force officers, Barron (1957) found the following coefficients of correlation between his measure of originality and various masculinity-femininity scores when Concept Mastery Test scores are partialed out:

Strong Vocational Interest Blank: Masculinity............ —.31
Minnesota Multiphasic Personality Inventory:
   Masculinity-Femininity .... .33
Personal Preference Survey: Feminine Identification........ .30

All the above relationships are significant at the .05 level and support the hypothesis that among males the more original individuals tend to be more feminine in expressed interests than the less original ones. In interpreting these findings, Barron suggests that perhaps women who do the kind of creative work usually done by men may show some degree of reversal of the usual sexual identifications. Barron cautioned, however, that his finding might be in part an artifact of his sample of military officers, who were on the average more masculine than men-in-general, and that high scores on femininity represented quite unremarkable deviations in the feminine direction.

In the present study, an attempt was made to explore tentatively the hypotheses suggested both by Roe (1959) and by Barron (1957), using a sample of gifted chemistry students and a sample of school counselors.

PROCEDURES

Subjects. The subjects of the study were 70 school counselors (57 men and 13 women), all attending the University of Minnesota Summer Guidance Institute.

Assessment Devices. Three instruments are of interest: (1) the Minnesota Multiphasic Personality Inventory, (2) the Strong Vocational Interest Blank, and (3) a Test of Creative Thinking. Only the masculinity-femininity scales of the Minnesota Multiphasic and the Strong were used from these two instruments. (Both men and women were administered the Men's Blank.)

The Test of Creative Thinking was developed by the author for use with this special group. Six of the eleven subtests were taken from general tests of creative thinking developed earlier by the author and the other four were designed to elicit creative thinking related to the problems of the school counselor. This battery of tests included:

1. The Ask-and-Guess Test. This test consists of three tasks and requires the subject (1) to think of questions concerning the behavior shown in a picture of Tom the Piper's Son stealing a pig, (2) to list possible causes, and (3) to list possible consequences. (Time limit: five minutes for each part.)

2. Improvements. Think of the most interesting and unusual ways you can to improve the toy dog (displayed) so that it would be more fun for a child to play with. (Time limit: eight minutes.)

3. Unusual Uses. Using the same toy dog, think of interesting and unusual uses for it other than as a toy. (Time limit: five minutes.)

4. Uses of Common Object. Think of interesting and unusual uses of tin cans. (Time limit: five minutes.)

5. Impossibilities. List as many practical impossibilities as you can think of relative to the education and counseling of intellectually gifted high school students. (Time limit: five minutes.)

6. Problems. List as many problems as you can think of which might grow out of each of the following two conditions: (a) an extremely permissive high school principal; (b) special high school classes for the intellectually gifted. (Time limit: five minutes.)

7. Improvements. List as many improvements as you can think of for the counseling and guidance of intellectually gifted high school students. You need not be concerned about the cost of these improvements or about other barriers to their implementation. (Time limit: five minutes.)

8. Uses. List as many uses as you can think of for the following principle as a guide in counseling intellectually gifted high school students: "Moderate stress continued over a prolonged period of time is more damaging to personality or mental health than brief periods of intense stress." (Time limit: five minutes.)

9. Consequences. What do you think would happen to education, if all curricula, programs of counseling and guidance, administrative procedures and the like were planned upon the basic premise that *all children and youth have limitless potentialities were they released by what is taught and the way it is taught?* Make as many speculations as you can concerning the consequences of such a condition. Do not feel bound by what now exists or is now possible. (Time limit: five minutes.)

Interscorer reliabilities of .90 or above have been established for all the subscores. The total score was obtained by adding the following subscores: ideational fluency, spontaneous flexibility, adequacy of response, inventiveness, constructiveness, curiosity, causal hypotheses, consequential hypotheses, sensitivity to problems, and sensitivity to emotions. Total scores ranged from 81 to 358 with a mean of 175.

RESULTS

Three scores were available for each counselor: the creativity score, the masculinity-femininity score of the Minnesota Multiphasic Personality Inventory, and the masculinity-femininity score of the Strong Vocational Interest Blank. Since the correlations between the masculinity-femininity measures and the creativity score were not significant and since scatter analysis suggested that a different set of relationships exists in the upper and lower halves of the distribution on the creativity score, the 57 males were split at the score which approximately divided the group in half. Product-moment coefficients of correlation were then calculated between the creativity scores and the two masculinity-femininity scores for each of the two groups. The results were as follows:

	r for M-F on MMPI	r for M-F on SVIB
High Creative Males (N = 29)............	−.38*	.28
Low Creative Males (N = 28)............	.21	−.21

*Significant at .05 level.

On both measures the relationship takes opposite directions in the high- and low-creative groups. In other words, among the highly creative males, the higher the creativity score the more masculine are the M-F scores; among the low-creatives, the higher the creativity score the less masculine are the M-F scores.

The coefficients of correlation were then transformed to Fisher's t score and the difference between the two correlations (high and low creatives) was tested for significance for both of the masculinity-femininity variables. The difference on the MMPI measure was significant at less than the .05 level and for the SVIB measure at between the .05 and .10 level.

Although there were only 13 females in the sample, product-moment coefficients of correlation were computed between their creativity scores and their scores on the masculinity-femininity measures with the following results: M-F on MMPI, $r = .36$; M-F on SVIB, $r = .24$. Since high scores for women run in the masculine direction, there is a consistent tendency for the creativity scores of the women in this sample to be related to the masculinity-femininity scores in the direction of the opposite sex. The relationships are not statistically significant with such a small number of subjects.

Since students of the Minnesota Multiphasic Personality Inventory have long insisted on the importance of patterns of scales to understand personality dynamics and since the masculinity-femininity scale is recognized as representing a complex variable, the profiles of the men were coded according to the MMPI codebook for counselors by Drake and Oetting (1959). According to Drake and Oetting, high masculinity-femininity scores with low scores on the social introversion scale are usually found among highly independent persons. High masculinity-femininity scores along with high scores on the hypochondriasis, depression, and/or hysteria scales are an indicator of dependency. Drake and Oetting also hypothesize that high masculinity-femininity scores serve as a control over aggressive or nonconforming patterns. Following the principles of coding suggested by Drake and Oetting, two sets of patterns on high (T scores of 55 or above) masculinity-femininity scorers were identified: (1) an independent group having low scores (T scores of 45 or below) on the social introversion scale and having its highest scores on the aggressive or nonconforming scales such as psychopathic deviate and manic; (2) a dependent group having its highest scores on the scales of the neurotic triad or psychasthenia. Eighteen of the males met the criteria for the independent group and 16 for the dependent group. The other males either had masculinity-femininity scores below 55 or had mixed patterns of independence and dependence as defined above. The mean creativity score of the independent group is 200.22 and the mean of the dependent group, 147.44. This difference is significant at the .001 level ($t = 3.951$).

DISCUSSION

There are several possible explanations of the findings reported above. One of the most obvious is that the meaning of high masculinity-femininity scores may differ considerably, depending upon what patterns accompany them. Since creativity requires both sensitivity (a feminine characteristic in our culture) and independence (a masculine characteristic), it is only reasonable to expect that high creativity is more likely to be found among individuals high on the masculinity-femininity scale and at the same time high on other scales that combine with it to make a pattern of independence than among those high on masculinity-femininity but high on the scales that combine with it to make a pattern of dependence.

Another possible explanation may be derived from the unusual nature of this group (highly feminine) and Barron's group (highly masculine). Barron (1957) recognized this possibility in explaining his results when he commented that his sample of Air Force officers were on the average more masculine than men-in-general and that high scores on femininity represented quite unremarkable deviations in the feminine direction. In a less masculine group, perhaps already screened for their sensitivity, the results are different. Since all probably have a high degree of sensitivity in the highly creative group (top half), the dominant factor is the independence and aggressiveness and the recessive factor is the sensitivity. The reverse tends to operate in the lower half.

John Anderson (1959) has discussed an analogous phenomenon in relation to ability levels. He believes that we should think in terms of thresholds and then consider the factors that determine function beyond this threshold. He cites as an example a motion picture firm which attempted to use selective devices in choosing chorus girls. Beauty was assumed to be the significant variable, but all the girls who applied were beautiful and beauty did not discriminate. Dancing ability did not discriminate either, because the applicants were all capable dancers. An intelligence test, however, gave significant predictions since the brighter girls could learn new routines rapidly and thus meet the changing demands from picture to picture and scene to scene. Beauty and dancing were both necessary, but once present in adequate degree, variance in another factor became important. Thus, sensitivity and independence are both important in creativity. Once either is adequate, variance in the other becomes important, or if both are adequate, something else becomes the determining variable.

In terms of the original hypothesis and previous research results, the most puzzling finding is the relationship between masculinity and creativity among the top half of the males on the creativity variable. Another possible explanation of this finding is suggested in Maslow's (1959) theory that the creative, self-actualizing person is able to integrate the various polarities within himself. It might be hypothesized that the more creative counselors have been able to integrate successfully the polarities of masculinity and femininity. Beyond the level of creativity represented by this top group, interests characteristic of one's own sex become a stronger determinant of creativity than the other way around. In other words, one is self-actualizing in the direction of the interests characteristic of one's own sex.

It will be recalled that Roe maintains that the conflict concerning sex-role identification is a persistent problem that plagues the highly creative individual. This, together with results from the author's own studies, suggests the need for studying this problem in the elementary and secondary school years as well as at the adult level. On the basis of the experience of the author and his colleagues, it seems likely that girls in the second and third grades are affected more seriously than boys by this conflict. Boys at the fourth, fifth, and sixth grade levels may be hit hard by these effects, however. These are problems for further investigation, since data thus far available are inadequate to provide answers.

SUMMARY

This exploratory study was made to test the validity of the hypothesis that highly creative persons tend to rate higher on masculinity-femininity scales in the direction of the opposite sex than less creative individuals.

Data were available on a group of 70 school counselors (57 males and 13 females). All had been selected after considerable screening for the University of Minnesota Summer Guidance Institute. Scores on the masculinity-femininity scales of the Minnesota Multiphasic Personality Inventory and the Strong Vocational Interest Blank and scores from a battery of tests of creative thinking were available for each counselor.

Among the males as a group, there is no statistically significant relationship between the creativity score and either of the masculinity-femininity scores. By splitting the 57 male counselors at the median on the creativity measure, a tendency was found in the top half for creativity to be related to masculinity and in the lower half to be related to femininity on both the Minnesota Multiphasic and the Strong measures of masculinity-femininity. The differences in direction are statistically significant. Two patterns of high masculinity-femininity scores were identified: one associated with independence (low social introversion, high manic, high psychopathic deviate) and one associated with dependency (high on the neurotic triad, high on psychasthenia). The mean score of the independent-feminine group was 200.22 on the test of creativity compared with a mean of 147.44 for the dependent-feminine groups (significant at the .001 level).

Among the 13 females there is a tendency for the more creative to be more masculine than the less creative, but the relationship is not statistically significant with such a small group.

Several possible explanations of the results were offered. The problem under study seems to be one worthy of research and one which needs to be studied in a variety of age and special interest or ability groups.

REFERENCES AND INDEX

REFERENCES

Anderson, J. E. 1960. "The Nature of Abilities," in E. Paul Torrance (ed.), *Talent and Education*. Minneapolis: University of Minnesota Press. Pp. 9–13.

Andrews, E. G. 1930. "The Development of Imagination in the Pre-School Child." *University of Iowa Studies in Character*, 3(4).

Ardleigh, J. D. 1959. "How to Get Profits — Not Problems from Creative People." *Management Methods* (Reprint).

Asch, S. E. 1955. *Studies of Independence and Submission to Group Pressure. I. A Minority of One Against a Unanimous Majority*. Swarthmore, Pa.: Swarthmore College.

Barron, F. 1957. "Originality in Relation to Personality and Intellect." *Journal of Personality*, 25: 730–742.

———. 1958. "The Psychology of Imagination." *Scientific American*, 199(3): 100–113.

Boroff, D. 1960. "American Colleges: What Their Catalogues Never Tell You." *Harper's Magazine*, 220: 33–40.

Bosselman, Beulah C. 1953. *The Troubled Mind*. New York: Ronald Press.

Buck, J. N. 1948. "The H-T-P Technique, a Qualitative and Quantitative Scoring Manual." *Journal of Clinical Psychology*, 5: 1–120.

Cattell, R. B., and J. E. Drevdahl. 1955. "A Comparison of the Personality Profile of Eminent Researchers with That of Eminent Teachers and Administrators." *British Journal of Psychology*, 46: 248–261.

Clark, C. H. 1958. *Brainstorming*. Garden City, N.Y.: Doubleday.

Compton, A. H. 1953. *Case Histories of Creativity: Creativity in Science*. New York: Industrial Relations Institute, Inc.

Drake, L. E., and E. R. Oetting. 1959. *An MMPI Codebook for Counselors*. Minneapolis: University of Minnesota Press.

Drevdahl, J. E. 1954. "An Exploratory Study of Creativity in Terms of Its Relationship to Various Personality and Intellectual Factors." *Dissertation Abstracts*, 142: 1256.

Flanagan, J. C. 1959. "The Relation of a New Ingenuity Measure to Other Variables." In C. W. Taylor (ed.), *The Third (1959) University of Utah Research Conference on the Identification of Creative Scientific Talent*. Salt Lake City: University of Utah Press. Pp. 104–123.

Getzels, J. W., and P. W. Jackson. 1962. *Creativity and Intelligence*. New York: John Wiley.

Goodenough, Florence L. 1949. *Mental Testing: Its History, Principles and Applications*. New York: Holt, Rinehart and Winston.

Gregory, J. M. 1886. *The Seven Laws of Teaching*. Boston: Pilgrim Press.

Guilford, J. P. 1959a. "Three Faces of Intellect." *American Psychologist*, 14: 469–479.

———. 1959b. "Intellectual Resources and Their Values as Seen by Scientists." In C. W. Taylor (ed.), *The Third (1959) University of Utah Research Conference on the Identification of Creative Scientific Talent*. Salt Lake City: University of Utah Press. Pp. 128–149.

———, and P. R. Merrifield. 1960. *The Structure of Intellect Model: Its Uses and Im-*

plications. (Report of the Psychological Laboratory, No. 24.) Los Angeles: University of Southern California.

Hebeisen, Ardyth A. 1960. "The Performance of a Group of Schizophrenic Patients on a Test of Creative Thinking." In E. Paul Torrance (ed.), *Creativity: Second Minnesota Conference on Gifted Children.* Minneapolis: Center for Continuation Study, University of Minnesota. Pp. 125–129.

Heck, D. L. 1958. *Some Uses of the Distribution of the Largest Root in Multivariate Analysis* (Mimeograph Series No. 194). Chapel Hill: Institute of Statistics, University of North Carolina.

Hiller, Roberta. 1961. "Your Ideas Are Important: An Experiment in Creative Writing." In E. Paul Torrance (ed.), *New Educational Ideas: Third Minnesota Conference on Gifted Children.* Minneapolis: Center for Continuation Study, University of Minnesota. Pp. 168–175.

Jex, F. 1959. "Negative Validities for Two Different Ingenuity Tests." In C. W. Taylor (ed.), *The Third (1959) University of Utah Research Conference on the Identification of Creative Scientific Talent.* Salt Lake City: University of Utah Press. Pp. 124–127.

Johnson, R. T. 1962. Unpublished Observations on Western Samoan Culture and Education. Minneapolis: Bureau of Educational Research, University of Minnesota.

Kendall, M. G. 1948. *Rank Correlation Methods.* London: Griffin.

Kubie, L. S. 1958. *Neurotic Distortion of the Creative Process.* Lawrence: University of Kansas Press.

L'Abate, L. 1957. "Sanford's Uncertainty Hypothesis in Children." *ETC.: A Review of General Semantics,* 14: 210–213.

Lecky, P. 1945. *Self-Consistency.* New York: Island Press.

Machover, Karen. 1948. *Personality Projection in the Drawing of the Human Figure.* Springfield, Ill.: C. C. Thomas.

Maier, N. R. F., and A. R. Solem. 1952. "The Contribution of a Discussion Leader to the Quality of Group Thinking: The Effective Use of Minority Opinions." *Human Relations,* 5: 277–288.

Maslow, A. H. 1959. "Creativity in Self-Actualizing People." In H. H. Anderson (ed.), *Creativity and Its Cultivation.* New York: Harper. Pp. 83–95.

――――. 1962. *Toward a Psychology of Being.* New York: Van Nostrand.

Mead, Margaret. 1939. *From the South Seas.* New York: William Morrow.

Merei, F. 1949. "Group Leadership and Institutionalization." *Human Relations,* 2: 23–40.

Miller, Joyce. 1961. "How to Talk to Children." *Home Life,* 15(11): 13.

Moore, O. K. 1961. "Orthographic Symbols and the Pre-School Child — A New Approach." In E. Paul Torrance (ed.), *New Educational Ideas: Third Minnesota Conference on Gifted Children.* Minneapolis: Center for Continuation Study, University of Minnesota. Pp. 51–101.

Moreno, J. L. 1947. *Psychodrama.* Beacon, New York: Beacon House.

Moustakas, C. E. 1959. *Psychotherapy with Children.* New York: Harper.

Mussen, P. H., and J. J. Conger. 1956. *Child Development and Personality.* New York: Harper.

Myers, R. E. 1960. "Creative Writing and Training in Divergent Thinking." Unpublished Master's Paper. Reed College, Portland, Oregon.

Osborn, A. F. 1957. *Applied Imagination* (3rd Revision). New York: Scribner.

Price, J. M. 1946. *Jesus the Teacher.* Nashville, Tenn.: Convention Press.

Quillian, M. R. 1957. "Creativity in American Life." *University of Chicago Magazine,* 50: 11–15.

Roe, Anne. 1956. *The Psychology of Occupations.* New York: John Wiley.

――――. 1959. "Personal Problems and Science." In C. W. Taylor (ed.), *The Third (1959) University of Utah Research Conference on the Identification of Creative Scientific Talent.* Salt Lake City: University of Utah Press. Pp. 66–77.

Rossman, J. 1931. *The Psychology of the Inventor.* Washington, D.C.: Inventors' Publishing Co.

Schafer, R. 1958. "Regression in the Service of the Ego." In G. Lindzey (ed.), *Assessment of Human Motives*. New York: Holt, Rinehart and Winston. Pp. 119–148.

Scheffe, H. 1953. "A Method of Judging All Contrasts in the Analysis of Variance." *Biometrica*, 40: 87–104.

Schenitzki, D. P. 1961. "Adult Evaluation and Peer Evaluation as Factors in Creative Thinking." In E. Paul Torrance (ed.), *New Educational Ideas*: Proceedings of the *Third Minnesota Conference on Gifted Children*. Minneapolis: Center for Continuation Study, University of Minnesota. Pp. 128–145.

Science Materials Center. 1958. *Science Toy Collection No. 2*. New York: The Library of Science.

Simmons, Virginia C. 1960. "Why Waste Our Five-Year-Olds?" *Harper's Magazine*, 220: 71–73.

Singer, J. L. 1961. "Imagination and Waiting Ability in Young Children." *Journal of Personality*, 29: 396–413.

Stein, M. I. 1956. "A Transactional Approach to Creativity." In C. W. Taylor (ed.), *The 1955 University of Utah Research Conference on the Identification of Creative Scientific Talent*. Salt Lake City: University of Utah Press. Pp. 171–181.

Sullivan, H. S. 1953. *The Interpersonal Theory of Psychiatry*. New York: W. W. Norton.

Taylor, C. W. 1960. "Identifying Creative Individuals." In E. Paul Torrance (ed.), *Creativity: Second Minnesota Conference on Gifted Children*. Minneapolis: Center for Continuation Study, University of Minnesota. Pp. 3–21.

Torrance, E. Paul. 1957. "Group Decision-Making and Disagreement." *Social Forces*, 35: 314–318.

———. 1961a. "Factors Affecting the Development of the Creative Thinking Abilities: An Interim Research Report." *Merrill-Palmer Quarterly*, 7: 171–180.

———. 1961b. "Can Grouping Control Social Stress in Creative Activities?" *Elementary School Journal*, 62: 139–145.

———. 1961c. "The Evaluative Thinking of Effective and Ineffective Teachers of Experimental Mathematics Courses." In E. Paul Torrance (ed.), *New Educational Ideas: Third Minnesota Conference on Gifted Children*. Minneapolis: Center for Continuation Study, University of Minnesota. Pp. 102–111.

———. 1962. *Guiding Creative Talent*. Englewood Cliffs, N.J.: Prentice-Hall.

———, and Kevser Arsan. 1961. "Effects of Homogeneous and Heterogeneous Grouping on Individual Behavior in Small Groups." In E. Paul Torrance (ed.), *New Educational Ideas: Third Minnesota Conference on Gifted Children*. Minneapolis: Center for Continuation Study, University of Minnesota. Pp. 51–66.

———, and J. E. Bowers. 1959. *Explorations in Creative Thinking in the Early School Years: Sex Roles and Appropriateness of Stimuli*. Minneapolis: Bureau of Educational Research, University of Minnesota.

———, and P. R. Krishnaiah. 1960. *Effects of Competition (without Practice) versus Practice (without Competition) on Fluency and Flexibility*. Minneapolis: Bureau of Educational Research, University of Minnesota.

———, and Janet Ross. 1961. *Improving Social Studies Education in Minnesota*. Minneapolis: Bureau of Educational Research, University of Minnesota.

Wallace, H. R. 1961. "Creative Thinking: A Factor in Sales Productivity." *Vocational Guidance Quarterly* (Summer 1961), 223–226.

Weinlander, Albertina A. 1959. *Your Child in a Scientific World*. New York: Doubleday.

Weisbord, M. R. 1961. "Let's *Not* Stifle Our Children's Creativity." *Parents' Magazine*, 36(11):48f.

INDEX